MEDITATIONS ON SELF-LOVE

MEDITATIONS
on SELF-LOVE

DAILY WISDOM FOR HEALING, ACCEPTANCE, AND JOY

LAURASIA MATTINGLY

ROCKRIDGE
PRESS

Interior and Cover Designer: Brian Lewis
Art Producer: Samantha Ulban
Production Editor: Andrew Yackira

Author photo courtesy of Madison Chertow.

ISBN: Print 978-1-64739-949-8 | eBook 978-1-64739-560-5
R0

*For my mother, Lourdes, my constant teacher
in life and now in spirit. For my father, Jack,
my own living Buddha.*

INTRODUCTION

I'm so happy you found your way here, to this book, and this moment. We're in an age of anxiety and live in a world where we are so hard on ourselves. I'm Laurasia Mattingly, a meditation teacher, and a student of life.

My own journey to self-love is a long and never-ending one, and meditation and mindfulness have become non-negotiables for me along the way. Both meditation and mindfulness have not only helped me heal from chronic anxiety and panic attacks, but also helped me overcome the deep grief I experienced after the loss of my mom.

I remember well the night my mom passed away. I saw her take her last breath as her soul left her body. That was the moment everything changed for me. It was a sad moment, but also peaceful because I realized she was no longer suffering. In that moment I knew there had to be more to life than what meets the eye. What used to be important to me no longer mattered. Her short life taught me that success isn't measured by how much I accomplished, but rather by how fully present and full of love I was each day. I learned that my mission here on earth is to share the importance and necessity of spreading love, to embody love and to walk in our truth, which is love.

After my mom passed, I worked with several mentors and spiritual teachers with decades of training and backgrounds in Buddhism, mindfulness, and tantra. Learning the ancient tools and techniques of meditation has helped me transform my life, and I'm happy to share them with you here in a relatable and approachable way. The teachings that I discuss everyday with my students are based in the Buddhist heart practices, which were created to ease the suffering of all beings.

A common thread among all the teachings, trainings, and silent retreats that I attended was the teaching of self-compassion, a quality where one learns to turn toward their own difficulties and care for them. Self-compassion is self-love. Before I found meditation, I used to run from my problems, take medication to numb the anxiety and depression, and pretend everything was fine and dandy. It was self-love that taught me to love all of myself fully, on the good days, and most important, on the bad days. My passion is sharing the tools and techniques that worked for me so that you, too, can find peace, ease, and love within yourself.

This book is filled with daily anecdotes of stories, teachings, and tools to help you find your way back to loving yourself. I encourage you to use this book in a way that works best for you. You may read entries in order, one per day, or flip to any page and find a lesson that resonates. You may also pick a specific topic from the index and go from there. The important thing to know is that there is no right or wrong way to use these meditations. The fact that you picked up this book and are reading it now means that you are already taking a step in the right direction, toward self-love.

1. WE ARE ALIVE!

What a gift it is to be alive! As humans we become so consumed with our difficulties that we often forget to celebrate the miracle of our aliveness. Being human is the greatest gift. To be able to breathe, feel, and experience the world is something worth celebrating every day. We wake up and our minds automatically begin to sort through our to-do lists, our problems, our distractions. Let us wake up and celebrate our precious lives. Feel the air on your skin, the breath in your lungs, the beating of your heart. Feel your aliveness and celebrate. We are alive!

> As you breathe, begin to sense your aliveness, your heartbeat, your vitality. Rejoice in being alive. Rejoice in this gift of being human.

2. PUT DOWN THE HEAVY LOAD.

Our difficulties weigh heavily on the heart. Sometimes difficulties consume us and we feel it. It's all we think about, or we feel it physically in the body. Sometimes we are unaware that they consume us, and it spills out into our lives, in the way we speak, the way we act, the way that we are. I once had a meditation teacher on a silent retreat ask the class, "Who said you have to carry it? Put it down." This is something I have to remind myself of often. If we are the ones choosing to carry the load, we are the ones who can choose to put it down.

> Sense what is weighing heavy on your heart. As you breathe, imagine the heaviness being lifted. Feel the gift of lightness.

3. COME BACK HOME.

Turning inward can be scary, especially if we don't love what we see. When I first started meditating, I was afraid to turn inward because I knew anxiety and depression were living inside me. I thought those emotions were "wrong." But I've learned there is no "right" or "wrong" way to feel. There is just being human. We are feeling humans who experience the full texture of life. We feel joy, sorrow, and everything in between. Our mindfulness is a refuge, a place where we can exist exactly as we are. So let us learn to come back home to ourselves, whatever that looks like and however that feels.

> May I accept myself as I am today. May I learn to love and accept myself unconditionally. I'm here, I'm home.

4. WAKE UP TO JOY.

Joy is something we knew well as children, unconditioned by society, unconcerned with romance or our bank account. There is something so pure and innocent about children, how they can go from laughing to crying in just a moment's time. As we grow older, sometimes we forget that this joy lives inside of our hearts. We take life and all its parts so seriously. Joy is nothing new. Joy is a remembering, a waking up. We might have forgotten, but let us remember. Joy has always been here and will always be here. We just have to look.

> Bring to mind a moment today that made you smile or laugh. Repeat to yourself silently, "May I remember my joy."

5. WE HAVE NOTHING TO HIDE.

We hold ourselves back for fear of rejection or getting hurt. It's a very natural human thing to do. But when we hold ourselves back, we do ourselves a disservice. We must learn to fully be ourselves. I find myself hiding parts of myself that I think others won't like, but then I begin to notice how I feel caged and not fully myself. We must learn to uncage ourselves and be our full, beautiful, unique, perfectly imperfect selves, unashamed. We won't be everyone's cup of tea, and that's okay, but we must remember to be our own!

Today, may I hold nothing back. Today, may I be myself fully. Today, may I remember I have nothing to hide.

6. CONNECTION.

We've all been given a unique set of DNA, a unique thumbprint, and a unique tongue print. One special gift of being human is that we are individuals. Individuals with unique bodies, hearts, and souls. We have different interests, passions, and morals. Yes, we are unique, but we are also one. We are connected to one another in more ways than you or I could count. But one thing every being on this planet has in common is the desire to be happy. Your best friend, your worst enemy, all the fish in sea—all share the desire to happy. This desire connects us; it makes us one.

Sit quietly and contemplate what makes you special and unique. Bring to mind your desire to be happy and remember that you are not alone.

7. WE'RE DOING OUR BEST.

We are all doing the best that we can in the moment, given the circumstances of our lives. We are all different people leading different lives. Sometimes people act or speak unskillfully, and we are hurt or offended. When we take things personally, we suffer. We must remember that we don't know anyone else's inner world. We only know our own. So the next time someone's words or actions hurt us, remember we're all doing our best together in this thing called life.

> Close your eyes and bring to mind a person who caused you pain. Realize that this person was doing the best they could in the moment.

8. WE ARE ALWAYS GUIDED.

We should learn to surrender to life, and trust that we are being guided on our paths, whatever those paths may be. Learning to surrender to life isn't always easy, especially when the going gets tough. But in those tough moments when we lose all hope, life somehow proves to us that we are supported. Proof of this is in the moments when we fell down but got back up. The heartbreak that we thought would last forever but didn't, the moments we cried so deeply but then found a smile. Let us surrender so we can be guided.

> Center yourself and as you breathe, begin to sense this unspeakable force that is guiding you. May you remember that you are always guided.

9. WHAT WE ARE TAUGHT.

As we are growing up, we learn so much from our parents, our peers, and our environment, both consciously and sub-consciously. When we are children we take in what we see and hear. But as we grow older we form a more solid sense of identity and individuality. I always find it quite fascinating how we are beautiful blends of what we are taught and our own uniqueness. Some things we may like and decide to carry with us, while those things we don't like are left behind. We have the power to create who we are while being influenced by what we are taught.

> Close your eyes and notice where in your life you do things for you. Notice where in your life you do things because it is what you were taught.

10. BE WHERE YOU ARE.

Comparison is a losing game. In today's society it's very easy to compare your path to another. Who has more success? Who has the best relationship? Who has more friends? There is no manual to life. There is no timeline or playbook for what you're supposed to be, do, or have. A flower just blossoms; it doesn't compare itself to its neighbor. Let go of how you think your life should be, and soften into how it is. Be like the flower; honor your blossoming, honor where you are, and love the ground upon which you stand. Be who you are in this moment; it's beautiful.

> May I let go of comparing my life to the lives of others. May I allow myself to blossom as I am and know that it is beautiful.

11. EMBODIMENT.

As a beginning meditation student, I attended all the classes, read all the books, and listened to all the podcasts, but I didn't feel my life changing until I stopped to notice the little moments of peace. When studying meditation, we learn to take notice of the moments of peace that the sages and teachers speak of. Like all things we learn in a classroom, these gleanings are for our highest good, but the real magic happens when we bring it out into the world with us. The same is true of our spiritual practice. Let us carry these teachings with us into the world.

> Center yourself and begin to notice if what you learn, say, and believe is in alignment with how you act. Practice embodiment today.

12. NOTICE WHAT WE AVOID.

As humans, when things get tough, we tend to avoid them. Of course we do—no one wants to experience a tough situation. But no healing comes from avoidance. I remember when my mother passed, I did everything in my power to avoid the sadness that was in my heart. But oftentimes what we avoid ends up becoming our greatest teacher. When I discovered meditation, I learned that emotions are always trying to teach us something. The sadness of losing my mother was teaching me to celebrate her memory, life, the air in my lungs, and the love in my heart.

> Center yourself and notice what emotions you've been avoiding. As you breathe, gently turn toward these emotions and let them teach you.

13. ACCEPT HELP FROM ANOTHER.

For some of us, asking for help comes easily; for others, learning the importance of asking for help, especially when it's needed, is a valuable lesson. We may think we need to be strong and figure it out all on our own. Some might view asking for help as a sign of weakness, but I can assure you it is a sign of strength. Asking for help is sometimes necessary, and there is value in getting the opinion or assistance of another. A set of fresh eyes, another open heart to understand, a pair of ears to listen. Let us be strong and ask for help when it is needed.

> May I ask for help when I need it. May I see the importance and gift of another being. May I see the strength in asking for help.

14. DISAPPOINTMENT.

Disappointment is a part of being human. Of course, we wish everything in our lives went according to plan, that we got all we deserved or desired, but that is not the case. We receive bad news, we get fired, we go through breakups, we lose a loved one—the list continues. We get stuck in the past, wishing things were different, or we try to distract ourselves, pretending that we don't care. What's needed instead is an embracing of this very natural human emotion. Disappointment teaches us that we humans have desires, and when they're not met, we hurt. It's okay to feel hurt.

> Close your eyes and bring to mind a moment of recent disappointment. Honor how this disappointment made you feel. Remember that however you feel is okay.

15. THE SPACIOUSNESS OF PERSPECTIVE.

In our minds, we so clearly think we know what's right. Even with our own lives and with ourselves, we think things are supposed to be a certain way. We cling to this ideal image. If we can give up our need to be right or for things to be perfect and look at a person or situation with fresh eyes, we experience a spaciousness. We're not lying to ourselves but rather reframing a situation, seeing something or someone in a new light. Oftentimes that new light can be very freeing. We need to stop clinging and see beyond.

May I see things in a new light today. May I realize that there is more than one way. Sense the spaciousness this new perspective offers.

16. WE MUST BE HONEST WITH OURSELVES.

Sometimes we find ourselves agreeing to things we don't want to do. People pleasers do whatever it takes to have everyone like them. Or if they act or speak in a way that they think people won't understand, they may feel like they must justify their words or actions. My teacher Mitra Manesh said, "It is better to gift someone with your absence than your presence full of resentment." When you don't want to do something or be somewhere, people can tell. Give everyone, including yourself, the gift of honesty. It'll be worth it.

May I honor myself today. May I honor my true feelings. May I give myself the gift of honesty.

17. TAKE THE RISK.

You'll never know if you don't try. In whatever way our lives unfold, somewhere along the path we will encounter a moment in which there is tension—a moment when our outer world doesn't feel in alignment with who we are. In the same way, if there's tension inside of ourselves, we're bound to encounter something in our lives that will force it out. We must take the risk to be who we really are in order to live our lives truthfully. Our lives cannot be wasted by avoiding conflict, because on the other side of risk is often a beauty that we would not have otherwise known.

> Breathe deeply and understand that being your true self is worth it in the long run. Know that the truth is worth the risk.

18. BE KIND ANYWAY.

Kindness is one of the greatest gifts we can give ourselves. It is also one of the greatest gifts we can give another. I can think of countless moments in my life where I was kind to a stranger for no reason and it made the person's day. The medicine of a smile or act of service goes a long way. "In a world where we can be anything, be kind" is a phrase that I try to embody every day. Of course there is always the option to be mean, rude, or angry, but what will always be remembered is your kindness.

> Center yourself and remember a time when you were kind for no reason. Recall how you felt, and how you made the other person feel.

19. LIFE'S CYCLE.

When I first began diving deep into meditation I went to a day-long meditation retreat with a well-respected teacher in the mindfulness world. She spoke of how the nature of our spiritual practice is a constant state of forgetting and remembering. Some days we experience the fruits of our meditation practice; we have a day full of peace, joy, and ease, and before we know it, we're losing our patience with a stranger or so stressed we lose sleep. This is all okay. Our lives ebb and flow. We might forget all we've learned and who we really are, but soon enough we will remember.

Close your eyes and feel a part of yourself you might have forgotten. As you breathe, remember that it will come back. It always does.

20. BE LESS UPTIGHT.

One of the greatest insights I had on silent retreat was that we suffer when our preferences aren't met. And wow, do we have a lot of preferences. I remember wishing the meditation hall was two degrees warmer, that the person next to me would breathe quietly, that the food had more salt. By thinking of these preferences and dwelling on how they were not being met, I was only causing myself to suffer. We humans like things to be a particular way. We must learn to let go a little and soften into the moment as it is. We must learn to be less uptight.

As you breathe, begin to notice the preferences you have in this moment. Soften and gently let them go. Let things be as they are.

21. YOU ARE NOT ALONE.

Oftentimes when we suffer, we feel alone. We think no one gets it. Yes, our problems are unique to some degree, but they are also problems that all humans face. When I lost my mother, I didn't think anyone knew how I felt because those who comforted me had never lost a parent. But whether it is the loss of a parent, a friend, a pet, or going through a breakup, we have all experienced loss in some capacity. Emotions rise and fall in all human beings. The circumstances may look different, but the feelings are the same.

Realize where in your life you have felt alone in your suffering. As you breathe, realize that you are not alone.

22. SEPARATION FROM LOVE.

One of my favorite authors and teachers explains that judgment is just a separation from love. When we judge others, or even ourselves, we are far from our true and kind and loving nature. Judgment diminishes our chances for joy. As a teen, I used to be so judgmental of other people's actions. I was far from love. As I grow older and meet people with kindness and allow for different thoughts, opinions, and actions that are different from my own, I open myself up to love.

Notice where in your life you tend to judge other people. Today, let go of judgment, and open yourself up to the love that is here.

23. TO BE SEEN AND HEARD.

We all have a desire to be seen and heard. We strive to be at the top of our class, to get attention from our peers, or be the best dressed at an event. These qualities are nothing to be ashamed of, as they speak to our innate human desire to be seen and heard. Let us meet our desire to be acknowledged with love.

Consider the common human desire to be seen and heard. Notice how you share this with the world. What is your intention behind it all?

24. WHAT IS "RIGHT" IN THIS MOMENT.

Isn't it funny how we always ask each other "what's wrong?" The human mind innately fixates on whatever it is that's bothering us and seems to skip right over all the things around us that are going well. This is why we can be having a wonderful day and then we get one annoying email and it's all we can think about. The way we humans can actually rewire our brains is by savoring what is going well and what feels good. Let us learn to ask each other, "what is right?"

Close your eyes and as you breathe, ask yourself, "What is right in this moment? What is going well?" Settle into and savor that feeling.

25. LOVING OURSELVES.

We must love ourselves. We must befriend ourselves. We must be able to come home to ourselves. Loving ourselves requires strength, courage, and understanding. Before I found meditation, I used to love myself conditionally. I loved myself only on the days when I felt joyful, peaceful, and happy. But this was not love. Love is like a gentle rain. It doesn't pick and choose where to rain and not to rain; it just rains. This is how we must love ourselves. Love is unconditional, without bounds. We must love ourselves through it all. On the good days, the bad days, and everything in between.

Center yourself and notice what parts of yourself you consider unlovable. Let your love be like rain and let it permeate every cell in your body.

26. WE MUST LOVE OURSELVES FIRST.

There is no greater feeling than being of service to others. It's what lights up my heart. But I've learned that I cannot help others when I feel empty or depleted myself. It's like when you're on a plane and the flight attendant tells you to put on your own mask first before assisting others. We must fill our own cup first, then fill others with the overflow. Once I began living this lesson, I was able to show up in the world more present, kind, and honest.

Close your eyes and notice where you feel depleted. With each breath, fill your heart with love. Once you feel full, share that love with others.

27. BE AUTHENTIC.

When we put ourselves fully out to the world as we really are, we live in our truth. I've struggled with this for many years. I was afraid of sharing parts of myself, fearing rejection. Meditation allowed me to get real with myself, and honor how I actually feel in the moment instead of striving to feel how I thought I was supposed to feel. When we show up in the world authentically, people are moved, whether they admit it or not. Give the world the gift of being your true, authentic self.

> May I honor how I actually feel today. May I no longer hide parts of myself for fear of being unlikeable. May I show up authentically.

28. ALIGN YOURSELF.

There is no better feeling than being in alignment. To me, alignment is when my inner and outer worlds meet in a way that I cannot put into words. When the body and mind fuse together and we feel whole. There is no us versus them. There is no separate self. There is just life. It's when you feel the Oneness that so many spiritual teachers describe, the connectedness that holds the world together. When our inner world does not mesh with our outer world, our lives don't feel real, or we feel numb or restless. Let you inner and outer world meet in your being and doing.

> Soften into yourself and let the world melt into your heart. Let the way you live your life be in alignment with your heart.

29. ALONENESS.

Find the power in your aloneness and you'll never be lonely. This is a lesson I am still learning. The risk to be in solitude, to become intimate with your own thoughts and feelings, to really get to know yourself, is true power. When we are alone, we begin to experience the true magic of life. We experience the magic of being fully present. I used to think loneliness and aloneness were the same thing. Loneliness is solitude without love, while aloneness is solitude with love. Infuse love into your moments of solitude and your world will change.

> Find a moment to be alone today. As you breathe, infuse this moment of solitude with love. With each breath, feel the power that is present.

30. THE JOURNEY OF TRANSFORMATION.

Every step you've taken has led you to this moment, right here and right now. Take a moment to honor how far you've come. When I think of my life, I realize it is a constant state of becoming, taking steps blindly into the unknown and growing as I do, sometimes without even realizing it. It's like the journey of a butterfly, beginning as a caterpillar and then making its chrysalis, and then waiting patiently and growing until it is strong enough to break out of that chrysalis and turn into the beautiful butterfly that was always within.

> Take a moment today to reflect on how far you've come. Realize that in every moment you are becoming who you were meant to be.

31. LOOSEN YOUR GRIP.

We cling so tightly to life. We cling to people, feelings, and labels that we think define us and make us who we are. But this is an illusion. Our being is not defined by what we have, how we feel, or what we do. But unfortunately, clinging causes suffering. We cling to a person and then they leave, we identify with our job title and then we are fired, and we cling to joy and then experience sadness. Our tight grip around life interferes with its natural flowing nature. We must loosen our grip and soften into life as all things rise and fall.

Center yourself and scan the body for any areas of tightness. As you breathe, begin to soften and loosen your grip around life.

32. SLOW DOWN.

Before I found meditation, I never appreciated the sensation of the sun warming my face, the sounds of the birds in the morning, or the wetness of the grass on my bare feet. Meditation continues to teach me to slow down to the speed of life. Slowing down is something I equate to waking up. So many of us live our lives asleep, numb, stuck in the busyness of our day-to-day, our minds consumed with regrets of the past or fears of the future. We must wake up to the present moment and open our eyes to the beauty of now.

Go outside and close your eyes. As you breathe, feel the sun warming your face. Notice the sounds of life happening around you.

33. WHAT WE HAVE IN COMMON.

The scientific fact that the human heart has the ability to sync with another heart means we share a common bond. Proof of this is in those moments when we meet a stranger and feel as if we've met them before, or when we are called to be kind to a stranger for no reason at all. Every human has kindness and love in their heart, and the universe knows this well. This is why kindness is rewarded—we are showing the world that we understand this commonality in all and we are awake to the true nature of being human.

Close your eyes and feel the beating of your heart. Allow your awareness to expand and contemplate that this beating heart is in everyone.

34. WHAT WE DESIRE.

Longing is an emotion that pulls us from the present moment. It's a wishing that the present moment was different from how it is; that something, someone, or some feeling that is not here now was here. Desires are a natural part of being human, and we can honor that. But we must not let our desires cause us suffering. We must acknowledge our desires kindly, and then return to the beauty of the here and now. Longing is like trying to fill a void. When we realize there is no void and that we are whole, we return to our true nature of love in the present.

Center yourself and sense the longing in your heart. As you breathe, remember that you are whole. Realize the present moment is full of love.

35. UNDERNEATH IT ALL.

When life gets difficult, I almost always delve into trying to think things through rather than feel the feelings that surface. This is the natural tendency of the human mind, to think our way to safety or clarity or peace. But this rarely works. Most of the time, if you simply allow yourself to feel the feelings and then meet them with kindness, they will fall. Our minds tell us otherwise. When we drop down from the mind and into the heart, we realize there is nothing to figure out, no problem to solve. Only feelings to feel, and life to live.

> Center yourself and slowly unhook from the thinking mind. Allow your attention to gently land in the heart, feel what's there, and meet it with kindness.

36. THE JOY OF OUR JOURNEY.

Our life is a never-ending journey. We learn so much about the world and ourselves along the way. We get so fixated on the destination that we forget to enjoy the journey. Not to say that we shouldn't have dreams or goals (we should); but rather, that we should take a breath and embrace where we are on our journey of life. Rather than being so focused on what lies ahead, let us soften into the here and now. We learn so much on the journey that ultimately makes us who we are when we reach our destination. But really, the journey is the destination.

> Take a breath and let go of your ideas of an imagined future, and drop into the beauty of where you are in your journey.

37. WHAT WE CARRY.

There is a fine line between empathy and taking on the pain of another being as your own. I was adopted, and the stories of my birth mother were alarming. I worked with several healers who told me that so much of the unworthiness I experienced was inherited from her. I felt hopeless, like this was the path intended for me because it was in my blood. I realized that because this was her life, it didn't have to be mine. I realized that, yes, I sensed her trauma in my being and felt that I carried it, too, but it didn't have to define who I was.

> May I realize that the pain of others doesn't have to be mine. May I have compassion and empathy for others without being controlled by it.

38. FROM LACK TO ABUNDANCE.

We humans are always striving for something. Striving for more peace, more love, more success. It's like we are trying to fill some sort of void. But when we shift our attention away from what is lacking and soften into what is here right now, we realize that what we've been searching for all along is already here. If we focus on what is absent, it's an insatiable search that will never be enough. Of course, let us aspire to be more loving, kind, and successful. But let's not lose sight of what's already inside of us.

> Center yourself and notice what you strive for. As you breathe, realize that it is already there inside of you.

39. OBSTACLES.

Suffering from debilitating anxiety as a teen and into my early twenties, I always viewed it as an obstacle to my happiness. Anxiety was in the way, but it became my greatest teacher. When I found meditation, anxiety was a frequent visitor. I would stress about plans or try to control my future. As I sat with the anxiety, I realized I needed to let go of control, go with the flow, and trust in life. Anxiety still arises in me, but rather than seeing it as an obstacle, I see it as something showing me the way.

As you breathe, notice what seems to be an obstacle to your happiness. With each breath, see that it is showing you what you need to learn.

40. SHARING YOUR GIFTS WITH THE WORLD.

It took me 26 years to realize that the reason I was put here on this planet is to share my gifts with the world. This is why each and every one of us are here: We all have gifts to share with the world. The world needs those gifts that make you unique and special. So please, hold nothing back. Be yourself, and show the world exactly what it needs: you. Share your gifts with the world.

Center yourself and contemplate what makes you unique. As you go about your day, share this unique gift of who you are with the world.

41. DON'T OVERCOMPLICATE THINGS.

Humans love to overcomplicate things. I'm guilty of this, too. We receive a text that is simply words on a screen, but we try to analyze what they mean, the tone of the words, and what the person on the other side of the screen *really* means. Sometimes, though, we need to take things at face value. Very rarely do people actually have ulterior motives. And very rarely does it have to do with us. In overcomplicating, we cause ourselves pain. Overcomplicating reminds me of a Buddhist teaching about what people thought was a snake in the path, which made them afraid. But after looking closely at the "snake," they realized it was a rope.

Close your eyes and bring to mind a situation that has you feeling uneasy. Rather than overanalyzing the situation, take it for what it is.

42. LIVE MINDFULLY.

I describe mindfulness to my students as living awake and doing things with full attention. I find myself watching TV as I eat, or looking at my phone while watching a movie. I find myself walking from my car thinking about what I have to do for the day, and then reaching my destination and missing everything along the way. Mindfulness is paying attention to the present moment without judgment. Mindfulness is not only practiced on the meditation cushion but also in our way of living. We focus our full attention to the one thing we are doing, and in doing so, we're living awake.

Pick one task today to do mindfully, and do nothing else at the same time. Allow your mind and body to fuse together fully in the moment.

43. HOLD NOTHING BACK.

Once, after I stopped seeing someone I was dating, I remember thinking to myself how I wasn't sad. My best girlfriends told me not to worry, it was his loss, and all the normal supportive stuff best friends say. But it wasn't until I was teaching a meditation class about giving our emotions the stage to express themselves that I sensed disappointment rising to the surface. It was like a seed that had been planted and was trying to grow. By resting in a state of openness and holding nothing back, my true feelings rose to the surface.

> Close your eyes and allow your awareness to gently land in the heart. Give your emotions the stage. Meet what arises with a friendliness.

44. LOOK THROUGH THE EYES OF A CHILD.

How exciting is it that each moment is a moment we have not yet experienced? It's as if we're looking through the eyes of a child, amazed and in awe of anything and everything. As we grow older, we forget the miracle of a new moment. When we realize this miracle, it restores our aliveness and reawakens our sense of wonder in the world. This is how I try to live my life, to temporarily suspend my regrets of the past and worries of the future and see the moment with fresh eyes, as if looking through the eyes of a child.

> Center yourself and sense the newness of each moment: a new thought, a new sensation in the body, a new sound, a new feeling.

45. WHEN LIFE IS TOUGH, BE KIND.

When life gets tough, be kind to yourself. When we resist life's toughness, we suffer. When we meet life's toughness with love, transformation occurs. Rather than avoid our difficulties, let us care for them. Self-compassion and kindness are like a healing balm that we apply to our wounds. Just as a parent holds a crying child, we hold our difficulties. Parents don't judge; they just love. Kindness and love toward ourselves is the greatest gift we can give. Times of suffering are when we need our own love the most. Love yourself. Self-compassion is a warrior practice because it takes great strength to turn toward our difficulties. You, my friend, are a warrior.

Center yourself and notice what difficulties need your attention right now. Soften into whatever is currently weighing on the heart, and silently repeat, "I'm here. I love you."

46. PAIN TURNS INTO WISDOM.

Difficulties in life are inevitable. It's how we respond that changes our experience. When pain is met with resistance, there is suffering. When pain is met with love, it turns into compassion and understanding. This was true for me when my mother passed. I used to resist the sadness. I would do everything in my power to not feel the feelings I was having. I learned to meet this sadness with love and my life changed. Sadness is a very natural human reaction to loss. Embrace the sadness and it will transform into wisdom—wisdom of what it is to be human.

Close your eyes and notice what difficulties you are currently resisting. Gently turn toward these difficulties and meet them with love. Notice how that feels.

47. BREAKING OPEN TO LIFE.

Life is not trying to break you down. It's trying to break you open. It's waking you up to the full texture of life. Many of us view breaking open as something bad, scary, or vulnerable. But breaking open is a sign of awakening. You are no longer walking blindly through life, but fully awake. Let life break you open, bleed out, feel the 10,000 joys and 10,000 sorrows life has to offer. See the beauty in your vulnerability and see the wisdom in your breaking. You are getting closer to your truth. You are awake.

> Notice the tender parts of the heart. Rather than trying to hold the heart together, allow the heart to break open. You are awake.

48. HOW TO GET UNSTUCK.

We are only stuck if we judge our path. We humans are always in a rush, trying to complete things as quickly as we can. We think, "I should be healed by now," or "I should have the promotion by now," or "I should be in the relationship by now." We criticize our journey rather than honoring where we are on our path. The secret to life is realizing there is no "by now"; there is only now. So when feeling stuck, we must take a breath and realize there's nowhere else we're supposed to be except exactly where we are.

> Notice where you feel stuck. Center yourself, and as you breathe, realize you are exactly where you're supposed to be.

49. THE BEAUTY OF BECOMING.

There is something so magical about being human. Every day we get to know ourselves a little better. Our journey of healing is a never-ending one, and even on days when we think we haven't done much, or days when we feel like we're regressing, we're really just getting one step closer to who we really are. I used to judge my spiritual journey, thinking my path was linear, and that a step backward was something bad. There's that saying that for every two steps forward, we take one step back. This so beautifully describes our process of becoming. There is beauty in any steps back.

Even though progress doesn't always feel like progress, may I remember I am always progressing in my journey of becoming who I am.

50. EMBARRASSMENT.

Think of those times when we embarrass ourselves as moments when our inner world and outer world don't match. It's when we know something to be true but act or speak otherwise, or don't speak at all. That tight feeling in the chest, the face getting hot. We've just put ourselves out there expressing what we know to be true and it is not well received. Or we know something to be true and do not express it. This is the risk we take in honoring our truth. Understand that people will not always agree with our truth, and that is okay.

The next time embarrassment arises, express yourself and don't hold back. Know that it is just a sign you are being true to yourself.

51. OUR PAST DOESN'T DEFINE US.

Being adopted, I've struggled with feelings of unworthiness.
As a child, I used to think I was unwanted. But really what I've
learned is that I was so loved, wanted, and cared for by my
parents who adopted me, and my birth mother gave me up
out of love. Our past does not define us. The past is just a part
of our journey, and how we might feel about it in a moment
doesn't define who we are as a whole.

> May I realize that my past is just a part of my journey
> and doesn't define how my future will look. Let it be.

52. THE VOICE INSIDE OUR HEAD.

The voice inside our head is always judging our every word,
our every thought, our every action. It's that inner roommate
who's always telling you how they feel and what you're doing
wrong. That voice is our inner critic, and although it may seem
like it, it doesn't have bad intentions. Biologically, it's just
trying to keep us safe. When we notice our inner critic, we
must not take everything it says as truth; instead we need to
bring in our inner soother: the heart. Our thinking mind keeps
us safe, but our heart keeps us wise. Our hearts don't judge;
our hearts understand what it is to be human.

> Next time you notice your inner critic judging you,
> invite in your kind, loving, and nonjudgmental inner
> soother. Your heart knows and understands.

53. THERE IS NO USE IN RUSHING.

Life has a pace of its own. Each moment unfolds exactly as it does. I will never understand why we humans like to get in the way of life. I find myself doing this often. I try to rush in love and in life. My mind wants answers now! But we can't know anything except the present moment. When we try to rush before we are ready, we end up stumbling. A caterpillar will die if you help it out of its chrysalis. The caterpillar will break free on its own in time, and so will you.

> Notice where in your life there is a sense of urgency. With each breath, soften into the now. Slowly let go of your need to rush.

54. HEALING IS A LIFELONG JOURNEY.

My students always ask me how meditation healed my anxiety and depression. Many think of healing as getting rid of a condition that's causing discomfort, but, especially in the spiritual world, this couldn't be further from the truth. I explain that meditation didn't "heal" the anxiety or depression, but rather it taught me how to meet myself and approach those stressful and deeply sad moments with more spaciousness and kindness. Anxiety and depression still arise in me quite often, but rather than resisting, I allow them to simply be. This is why we are never "healed." As long as we are living and breathing, we are healing.

> As you breathe, realize each breath is a healing breath. As you feel, realize each emotion is teaching you something. You are healing.

55. SLOW DOWN.

Thich Nhat Hanh, a Buddhist teacher, author, and monk, often describes how we are so good at preparing to live but not very good at living. We are willing to dedicate years of our lives to get a diploma, a car, a house, etc., but waste the beauty of the present moment. When I find myself getting caught up in where I'm going, this teaching always helps me slow down. It allows me to savor where I am. We get too focused on results and comparing where we are on our path to others. Instead, let's enjoy the present moment.

Center yourself and notice what's here and now. Notice the sounds of life happening around you. Notice sounds as they rise and fall.

56. UNDERNEATH TRUTH IS BEAUTY.

Pema Chödrön, a Buddhist teacher, author, and nun, has a famous quote: "Fear is a natural reaction to moving closer to the truth." A lot of us are afraid of the truth. We lie to ourselves or others to keep what's really underneath buried because we're ashamed of the truth, or fear that we will be judged for speaking or living our truth. But on the other side of fear is freedom, because underneath the truth is beauty. We must overcome the fear of not living our truth so that we can be truly beautiful. The truth isn't always easy, but it is always beautiful.

Center yourself and sense any fear resting on the heart. Breathe and realize that underneath lies the beautiful truth of who you are.

57. WHAT GETS IN THE WAY.

What are you not saying or doing that is preventing you from feeling free? I find myself in this predicament often, where I'm ready to express how I really feel but then fear gets in the way. I'm learning that it's never worth letting fear take over. When I hold back my truth, it weighs heavily on my heart and makes me feel like I'm living a lie. What an injustice we do ourselves by allowing fear to get in the way of our true feelings. Sometimes we won't be agreeable, likeable, or loveable to others. What's important is that we are all of those things to ourselves.

Sit quietly and notice fear inside you. As you breathe, imagine this fear is not an obstacle but a bridge leading you where you need to go.

58. LIVE LIFE FOR YOU.

Why do so many of us live our lives for other people? We say we do things for our parents, our spouses, our generations before us. We say we have to, that it's our obligation, our duty, our mission. We must seek clarity on our intentions, because if we do things for others, we will never truly be happy. Happiness isn't found outside of ourselves; it's found in our hearts. This doesn't mean we can't be in service to others or do things for others. The intention behind our actions and efforts must be for our own hearts to blossom.

Center yourself and as you breathe, notice what your own heart wants. Is this reflected in what you do or say in the world?

59. HESITATION.

When we hesitate, we hold back our truth. To me, spiritual practice is learning to be myself fully without hesitation. To allow whatever arises to arise, to feel the feelings that want to be felt, to gently acknowledge the thoughts that come and go. Rather than questioning ourselves, let us breathe and remember that this is why we are all here: to live in our truth, to live out our most authentic and aligned lives. So please don't hesitate. Leap into your vastness without fear. It'll be worth it, I promise.

> Close your eyes, and sense if there is any hesitation present within you. Let each breath remind you that you are brave.

60. CONNECTED TO ALL.

We all want to love and be loved. If we look close enough we can see this. Sometimes we lose sight of this connection. We tell our own stories, using the distinct details and different circumstances of our lives to show how we are special or different. But at the end of the day, feeling separate from everyone and everything is a direct path to suffering. We must tap back into the connectedness and realize we are all one to feel complete. We must be careful not to live our lives in our own separate bubbles, and return to what connects us all: love.

> Close your eyes and sense your need to love and be loved. Know that this is the thread that connects us all.

61. THE ILLUSION OF CONTROL.

Control is an illusion. We think we can control a situation, a person, or how we feel in the moment. But this is not up to us. What we do have power over is how we choose to respond. We cannot control what happens in our life, how people will act, and how life will unfold. We can meet what arises in our lives with an open and understanding heart, realizing that this is what it means to be human, and from that place of acceptance, take action. We can respond rather than react. Let go of control and welcome in ease.

> Center yourself and notice where in your life you're trying to take control. As you breathe, soften and let go. Surrender to how life is unfolding.

62. LIFE IS TO BE LIVED, NOT UNDERSTOOD.

I am guilty of trying to think my way through difficult situations to arrive at an answer that cannot be known. I think all humans are guilty of this. We think that if we overanalyze this situation to death, we can land on an answer or find clarity. We do this in love, our jobs, and relationships. We try to decode actions, words, and the way things play out, looking for solidity in the unsolid nature of life. I'm coming to learn that life is to be lived, not understood. When we try to understand, we pull ourselves way from the present.

> Unhook from the thinking mind and drop into the heart. Stop trying to understand, and feel the present moment within you.

63. THE RISK OF PLAYING IT SAFE.

Many of us seek safety in preparing for an unknown future. We work endless hours to save money for retirement, we spread ourselves thin for vacation days we never use, we do so much to prepare to live. But by playing it safe, we may risk missing out on many memorable experiences. Before they adopted me, my parents spent all their savings on traveling the world. It was good that they did, because my mom ended up passing away at the young age of 54. Had they played it safe, they would not have had the wonderful experiences that made up so much of my mom's life.

Let go of your illusions of a safe, predictable future. As you breathe, soften into taking the risk of not knowing.

64. THE MIND CAN WANDER. JUST BRING IT BACK.

I once had a teacher who said meditation and training the mind is like training a puppy to sit. A common misconception in meditation is that we control our minds, that we stop our thoughts or slow them down. But really, meditation teaches us to return to the present with a friendliness. When training a puppy, if we use too much force or are too strict, the puppy will be scared to sit. When we train the puppy with a friendliness, it will want to sit. It's the same with our mind. We can let it wander, but gently and kindly bring it back, so the mind will want to be present.

Close your eyes, allow the mind to wander, notice the wandering, and gently bring it back to the present with a friendliness.

65. BEGIN AGAIN.

Sharon Salzberg, an incredible teacher, author, and meditator, said meditation is resilience training of the mind. It is a constant beginning again, beginning again, and beginning again. When our mind wanders, we simply begin again. This is why even Buddhist monks in Tibet with 30 years of meditation practice are called practitioners, not masters, because our mind is unknown. We cannot know what will arise until it arises. It's the same with our lives, off the meditation cushion. We have the ability to begin again in each moment. Living life is a practice.

> Center yourself and notice where in your life you feel stagnant. As you breathe, sense that you are beginning again.

66. UNCLENCH THE FIST.

We cling so tightly to the way we want ourselves and our lives to be. We cling to preferences, opinions of others, judgments, people, and our ideas of how we want things to be. It's like we're clenching life tightly in our hand, holding on to something that can't be held. Life isn't meant to be held onto. Life is about letting go, letting be, and softening into the way things are. Meditation practice is like the clenched fist unclenching. We open up to life as it is, and allow it to flow through us. Soften, let go, and trust.

> Center yourself and sense where you are holding on to life. As you breathe, soften and let go into how things are.

67. LIVE TRUTHFULLY.

We have a responsibility to ourselves to live in our truth. We must voice our opinions, express our feelings, and live truthfully; not for anyone else, but for ourselves. I'm learning this lesson still. In love, I find myself holding back, scared of saying the wrong thing, or being "too much." But if I live in my truth, I realize there is no wrong thing to say, and I'm not too much. By living in my truth, I attract all things and people that are in alignment with me and my vibration.

> May I give myself the greatest gift of all and live in my truth. May I do it for me, and no one else.

68. IMPERMANENCE.

We all are born, and we all must die. This is the harsh yet beautiful reality of being human. We cling to life and our youthfulness, but death is inevitable. Death may sound scary, but there's a reason many Buddhists contemplate death in order to experience happiness. When my mother died, I experienced impermanence firsthand. Her passing taught me to look at life in a new light. I realized life is short, unpredictable, and tomorrow isn't promised. Death isn't here to scare us; it's here to remind us to live.

> May I realize life's impermanent nature. May I remember tomorrow isn't promised. May I remember to live life fully.

69. WE ARE IN EVERYTHING.

We are in everything and everything is in us. Life is fluid and so are we. This was a shocker for me when I first started meditating. My teacher described how a flower is made up of many non-flower elements. The sky is in the flower, the soil is in the flower, the seed is in the flower, and we are in the flower. It is the same with our human bodies, made up of many non-human elements. Everything is in us and we are in everything. This is a contemplation and feeling rather than an understanding. When we realize that nothing is solid or permanent, we experience freedom.

Close your eyes and contemplate all of the non-human elements within you. As you breathe, realize you are in everything.

70. TRUST THE UNKNOWN.

We cannot know what lies ahead. All we can know is the present moment. The unknown is scary for most. Our minds so desperately want to guess at an unknown future. We humans shy away from uncertainty. But really, freedom comes when we begin to trust the unknown. It sounds silly to trust something that we don't know, but this is the secret to life. Peace doesn't come when we have total control; it comes when we realize we don't need it. The unknown is a beautiful and scary place, but it is what makes being human undeniable and indescribable.

May I learn to trust the unknown. May I soften into the uncertainty. May I be okay with not knowing what lies ahead.

71. THE BEAUTY OF TRUE FRIENDSHIP.

To see your own innate beauty reflected back to you in the form of another being is one of the greatest gifts of being human. This reflection is true friendship. When we're lost, friends help show us the way. When we feel unworthy, they remind us we are more than enough. When we are sad, friends are our shoulder to cry on. When we feel lonely, friends remind us we're not alone. When we're given the gift of true friend-ship, it's as if we've been given a mirror that reminds us of our own forgotten beauty.

Center yourself and bring to mind a true friend. Realize that this friend sees your beauty and is here to reflect it back to you.

72. FIND PEACE IN FAMILIARITY.

There is something peaceful and calming about hearing a song from our childhood or seeing longtime friends. Familiarity brings us peace in an ever-changing world. It's why so many people suggest creating a morning or bedtime routine for well-being. Familiarity grounds us when we feel overwhelmed or unstable. So let us savor the familiar moments, songs, people, and situations that arise in our day.

Close your eyes and bring to mind a pleasant moment in your past. Notice what in the present moment reminds you of this past moment.

73. HEALING TAKES TIME.

Healing isn't something that can be rushed. This lesson continues to be something I must accept. What drew me to meditation was the debilitating anxiety I used to experience as a teen and into my early adult years, and something I experience to this day. When I first dove deep into meditation and had several years of daily sustained practice over time, my anxious feelings began to subside. When I get anxious today, a moment of shame arises and my inner critic says, "you should be over this by now." But then I remember that healing is a lifelong journey.

> May I remember that healing takes time. May I remember that I am perfectly on schedule. May I remember that healing is a lifelong journey.

74. THE RISK OF PROTECTING OURSELVES.

Sometimes protecting ourselves holds us back. I find myself stuck in this predicament often, not releasing a piece of work for fear of it not being "ready" yet, holding back a piece of information for fear of offending someone, or not expressing my true feelings for fear of getting hurt. Sometimes we must choose between protecting ourselves and exposing our truth. We can stay safe and protected, but we may not be seen or heard in quite the way we hoped for. When we choose to expose our truth, we run the risk of being too vulnerable as a result of being honest. No one can make this choice for us; it is up to us alone.

> Bring to mind a difficult decision you have to make. As you breathe, allow your heart to tell you what to do.

75. GIVING TOO MUCH OF OURSELVES.

Boundaries are important. Giving to others can feel like a drug, and we get a high off the feeling of being in service to others. But sometimes we can give too much of ourselves. So much that it begins to eat away at our hearts, sometimes without us even realizing it. We start to put other people's feelings, happiness, and well-being before our own. But by doing this, we do a great disservice to ourselves. There is a strength in setting boundaries. Know when enough is enough and when to take a step back, rest, and refuel, so you can show up in the world as the best you.

> Center yourself and see where in life you have been giving too much of yourself. As you breathe, notice where boundaries are needed.

76. THE STRENGTH IN OUR SOFTNESS.

People are called "soft" when showing signs of sensitivity. What I've learned is that it takes strength to soften, that there is so much beauty in being vulnerable. Part of being human is having moments of vulnerability. So often we show up to life's moments with a harshness, thinking the best way is to power through. But more often than not, what's needed is to meet a moment, person, or situation with softness. We put up walls around our hearts thinking they are protecting us. But really they're preventing us from feeling the wholeness of life.

> Close your eyes and sense where you are meeting life with a harshness. As you breathe, soften. See how your softening is strong.

77. THE DANGER OF OVERTHINKING.

The mind can be our friend or our worst enemy. It's like pull-
ing a thread that has begun to unravel when we should leave
it alone. I have to catch myself when I begin to pull the thread
of worry about an imagined future. Overthinking pulls us from
the present. We think that if we could just control our future or
know what lies ahead, we will feel at ease. But this only causes
us to spiral into overthinking and anxiety. By remaining in the
present, there is nothing to analyze, only a moment to be lived.

> Center yourself and let go of trying to figure things out.
> Allow your attention to rest on a sound or sensation in
> the body that's happening in the present.

78. RUMINATION OR FREEDOM.

Ruminating in the past does us no good. Our mind rests in
wishing things could have turned out differently. We waste so
much time and energy trying to change the past that cannot
be changed. Or we cling to a beautiful memory in the past
that is no more. I'm not saying we can't have memories or
think of the past, but we must dip into the past lightly and
with discernment. Our rumination of the past pulls us away
from the present. It pulls us away from the beauty that is in the
here and now.

> May I visit the past with the understanding that the
> past is the past. May I allow my attention to rest in the
> present.

79. REST WHEN YOU ARE TIRED.

Resting when I'm tired is something I'm still learning to do. We live in a society where busyness seems to determine our level of success. But is this really success? Sometimes our bodies are tired and they need stillness, or our minds are exhausted and they need a break. We must remember that each and every one of us deserves rest. Perhaps this is why I was so drawn to meditation, because it was a place where my body, mind, and heart could rest. Honor yourself by resting when you are tired. Resting is not a sign of weakness; it's a gift you deserve to give yourself.

May I honor myself the next time I feel tired. I give myself the gift of rest, and allow my body, mind, and heart time to recharge.

80. THE BEAUTY OF NOT KNOWING.

Animals are the best reminder of living in the beauty of not knowing. House cats wake up not knowing what the day will hold and sunbathe without a worry in the world. Dogs wake up with wagging tails showing their humans unconditional love, trusting they will be fed and walked. I think we humans could learn a lot from animals. We tend to overcomplicate things. We try to know what cannot be known. But the lesson in watching animals and nature is trusting that the unknown in life will unfold exactly as it should.

Center yourself and as you breathe, trust that your life is unfolding exactly as it should. Trust the unknown.

81. LET JOY FIND YOU.

On cloudy days we can't see the sun, but we know it's shining on the other side. Sometimes we can't feel it, but knowing it's there brings us peace. This knowing is the same with joy. Sometimes in the present moment, we are overwhelmed with our difficulties and joy seems far away. But we must remember that even if we can't see it or feel it, joy is still there. Proof of this is those moments when you're crying and then start to laugh, or you're so stressed out and a piece of music makes you feel at ease. Joy is always there; we just have to look.

Close your eyes and sense what difficulties are weighing on the heart. Open up your awareness and know that joy is also there.

82. TO TRULY LISTEN.

Oftentimes when we are listening to someone talk, all we can think about is what we are going to say next. What piece of advice we can offer, or what we think we can improve about a situation. But to truly listen, we must listen without an agenda. We must listen only to listen. We listen so that another person can be truly heard. Even if the other person is asking for advice, let us listen without being clouded by our opinions and judgments. From that place of true listening, we can mindfully respond.

Practice deep listening today with another. Truly listen without thinking about what you want to say next or focusing on yourself. Allow someone to be truly heard.

83. FEEL THE FEELINGS THAT WANT TO BE FELT.

Feel the feelings that want to be felt. It sounds simple, but of course it's easier said than done. Oftentimes when someone asks us how we feel, we end up sharing the circumstances of our suffering, the things or people that caused the pain. But rarely do we feel what needs to be felt. Our natural human reaction to difficult feelings is to annihilate, evade, or void them, but no healing comes from that. These emotions are calling for our attention, and they want to be met by our presence. Thich Nhat Hanh said, "We must greet our feelings as we would greet a friend."

Close your eyes and notice what feelings are present in your experience. Simply meet them with kindness and feel them in your body.

84. BE YOU, UNAPOLOGETICALLY.

You are fluid; you are changing. You are not only a work of art but also a masterpiece! On some days you might be peaceful and kind, while on other days your fuse might be short and you might say something to a stranger that you regret. All of this is okay. I often find myself trying to act as a meditation teacher is "supposed" to act. And I shame myself for the moments where I am rude to someone on the road, or feel nonspiritual. Once we allow ourselves to be the walking contradictions that humans are, we give ourselves the freedom to be, unapologetically.

May I be myself unapologetically today. May I remember that being human is a walking contradiction, and that's okay.

42

85. LET GO OF THE "OLD" YOU.

Change is inevitable. Just like a caterpillar becomes a butterfly or a snake sheds its skin, we are constantly evolving. This letting go is part of something we as humans also must do in order to become who we truly are. No one said this change would be easy, or that it would be painless. In fact, usually the opposite is true. But change is necessary. Letting go of the old parts of who we are is scary and makes us feel vulnerable, but this is how we make space for what's to come. What's old must fall away.

> Close your eyes and notice a change in yourself that you've been resisting. Understand that in this letting go you will be transformed.

86. THE DISCOMFORT OF GROWTH.

There's a reason growing pains are called "pains." Growth is rarely a pleasurable experience. Even when our physical bodies are growing from children into teens and later into adults, our bodies literally hurt. The same is true of humans growing spiritually. Oftentimes it takes our toughest moments and lessons to be learned to truly grow. For me, love teaches the gift of growing, however painful that may be. Going through a breakup is rarely pleasurable and often painful. We feel the heart shatter. But from that dark moment, like a phoenix rising out of the ashes, we end up learning more about ourselves and love than ever before.

> Center yourself and notice where you feel discomfort. Find comfort in the uncomfortable, knowing you are growing into the person you are supposed to be.

87. SIMPLY BE.

Our minds are always trying to figure something out. Our bodies are always on the go. We humans are doers, but sometimes what's needed is no doing at all. Sometimes what we need is to simply be. Being with the breath as it rises and falls, being with the sounds of life happening around us, being with a sensation in the body as it comes and goes. Our soul longs for presence. Sometimes no answers come from doing. Like the Buddha said, "Quiet the mind and the soul will speak." The ultimate medicine is presence, and allowing ourselves to simply be.

Stop what you're doing and close your eyes. Feel your breath, notice the sounds around you, and sense your body. Allow yourself to simply be with what is.

88. BEING REAL WITH OURSELVES.

What I love most about meditation is that it forces us to be real with ourselves. Meditation isn't about how you want to feel or how you think you should feel, but rather it's unfogging the lens and seeing what's actually there. We might not always like what we see, but that's the beauty of presence: it's truthful. We so often look through a lens clouded with judgment or ideas of what we think life's supposed to look like or how we're supposed to feel.

Close your eyes and as you breathe, ask yourself, "How am I really?" Honor whatever answers come up, knowing you are being real with yourself.

89. WHAT HOLDS THE WORLD TOGETHER.

There is an invisible thread that holds the world together. The thread of love, the thread of existing, the thread of doing our work here on this earth every day. Every human being exists to do their part, but not because they are told to do so. This is simply the way of life; it's an unspoken rule that every human on this planet understands. Flowers start as seeds before they blossom, the seasons change, and humans are born and then die. The waves continually crash against the shore, the sun rises and sets. Everything that exists has a purpose and its own experience.

Close your eyes and feel this invisible thread of life. Contemplate how everything on this planet knows exactly what to do without question.

90. WE'RE ALL ON THIS JOURNEY.

Whenever I travel to a foreign country, I'm reminded of how similar people are despite their differences. Our language, our physical appearance, our way of life, our values, our morals— these are all very different from one another. But no matter where in the world I am, I remember that every one of us is on this journey of life together. My friends in Morocco, Bali, and Spain are all very different, yet all the same. Each of us wishing to be happy, each of us breathing the same air, each of us with beating hearts. Each of us journeying through life.

As you move through the world today, look at a stranger and realize that you are both on this journey of life together.

91. DON'T BE AFRAID OF SILENCE.

When in the presence of another being, I find myself trying to fill moments of silence with unnecessary words, as if silence is something to avoid. I used to view silence as a sign that the connection with another being wasn't strong or that some-thing was going wrong. But I'm learning there is power and beauty in silence. When two beings are comfortable with each other and no words need to be spoken, that's connection. If discomfort arises in the midst of silence, meet that dis-comfort with kindness. Savor the spaces between words and sense its beauty.

> When connecting with another being today, notice the moments of silence. See those moments as a gift, where no words are needed. That presence is more than enough.

92. WHEN FORGIVENESS IS NEEDED.

Part of being human is getting hurt or hurting others. I was 17 when my mother was diagnosed with stage 4 pancreatic cancer. I have memories of saying hurtful things to her. I suffered after her passing knowing that my words hurt her. I felt guilty, which was causing me to suffer more. We cannot change the past. Things happen, and people get hurt. What we can change is how we care for ourselves in the present. Letting go is needed, but the phrase "letting go" can be a bit confusing, because really what we are doing is letting be. With forgiveness we make amends with our hearts. We acknowledge the past, without being limited by it.

> May I forgive myself for hurting anyone knowingly or unknowingly out of confusion, ignorance, fear, or pain, for I am only human.

93. WE HAVE TO START SOMEWHERE.

There will never be the "right moment" or the "perfect time" to start. A saying that sticks so deeply in my heart is "begin where you are." We lose our way or hold ourselves back waiting for the illusion of the perfect moment to start. But we must remember we all have to start somewhere. Allow yourself to be a beginner. Give yourself the gift of simply starting, and take the first step, however scary it may be. Know that wherever you are on your path is exactly where you're supposed to be. Know that the perfect time and moment is now.

Imagine yourself as a seed being watered and blossoming without hesitation. The seed knows it's a flower even when it's a seed.

94. EXPRESS WHAT IS INSIDE.

We all have those moments where a feeling rushes over our body and we want to cry out—like when something is funny and we burst out laughing, or those moments of anger when we just want to scream, or times of sadness when we want to wail. I remember driving through a canyon on a cloudy day listening to a beautiful song when suddenly tears started streaming down my face. There was no reason for me to be crying other than my heart expressing what was inside. Feelings don't always need an explanation; they just need expression.

Center yourself and notice any feelings inside the heart, without trying to figure out why they are there. Soften and allow them to be expressed.

95. ALLOW OTHERS THE FREEDOM TO BE WHO THEY ARE.

Allow others to be who they are and allow yourself to be who you are. I believe that as we grow older, we form ideas of how people should think, speak, and act. As we grow up, we begin to care what other people think of us. Something I struggled with deeply as a teen and young adult was caring about what other people thought of me. But I've realized this fear of judgment and my own judgment of others only holds me back. Allow others to be as they are and give yourself the freedom to be you.

May I give myself the freedom to be myself fully today. May I give others the freedom to be who they are fully and without judgment.

96. WE ARE EVERYTHING AND WE ARE NOTHING.

Guru Nisargadatta Maharaj said, "Wisdom tells me I am nothing. Love tells me I am everything. And between the two my life flows." This quote always grounds me back into what it means to be human. Wisdom teaches us that the world is so much bigger than our own individual problems; it reminds us of our Oneness and connection to all. Yes, our being is vast and cannot be contained, and in the grand scheme of things we are a small speck amid a giant universe. Love teaches us that we are whole and worthy of everything we could ever want or need.

Close your eyes and sense that you are everything and nothing all at once. Feel the wisdom and love that rests within you.

97. DON'T LET LIFE PASS YOU BY.

In mindfulness, to be an observer is a good thing. It gives us space to take a step back so we can respond instead of react. But there is a fine line between being an observer and becoming indifferent. We risk life passing us by if we completely remove ourselves. If we become a watcher instead of someone who lives, bes, and does, we isolate ourselves from the world. We do ourselves a disservice by becoming indifferent or apathetic, or when we spend time analyzing life instead of living it. Jump in and live it before it's too late.

Close your eyes and allow yourself to observe and be. Make a promise to yourself today to fully live. Don't just watch.

98. COMING HOME TO OURSELVES.

The idea of coming home to ourselves is what meditation means to me. Meditation is a refuge, a place where I can close my eyes, turn inward, and be with my heart. Before I found meditation, I didn't want to come home to an anxious, depressed, unworthy self. But meditation reminds us that we are these human beings with feelings, and so, rather than becoming our own worst enemies, we must become our own best friends. We must learn to come home to our hearts no matter how they're feeling and love them anyway. Love yourself unconditionally so you can come home.

Center yourself and notice how the heart feels. As you breathe, know that it is safe to come home. It is safe. Come home.

99. LIFE'S PLAN.

It took my life's most difficult moment to have my most profound healings. It took my mom dying, and my heart shattering to learn that love is what matters most. There is always beauty in the breakdown. Sometimes it's hard to see that in the moment, but what feels like your lowest self is making way for your highest self. The universe doesn't give you what you can't handle; it gives you what you need to learn. Life isn't trying to break you down; it's trying to break you open to life, showing you you're fully awake to life. Break open.

> Close your eyes and sense where in your heart you feel you're about to break. Rather than trying to stop it, let it break open.

100. SPEAK YOUR TRUTH.

Even if no one is listening, speak your truth. If one person listens, you've made a difference. In choosing to not speak, we put ourselves in a self-contained prison, and we cause our own suffering. Speak your truth; don't trap yourself in a cage. Take the risk of being rejected, challenged, or silenced, knowing that at least you spoke your truth. When I first began teaching at 25 years old, I doubted myself. Who would listen to a 25-year-old share lessons on life? I have had more than 10,000 students of all ages, from 5 to 85 years old, tell me I helped them.

> Close your eyes and sense a truth you are holding back. Notice how that imprisons your heart. As you breathe, vow to speak your truth.

101. HONOR IT ALL.

Bow to every step you've taken to get to where you are today. Bow to the leaps and bounds you've made—the missteps, too. We must honor every part of our journey. We tend to only celebrate the wins, but did you ever consider that even the losses are wins? We must celebrate it all and honor everything, or we will get stuck in the illness of only loving ourselves when we're at our best. Conditional love is not love at all. Honor your journey fully and completely; it is what makes you the unique and beautiful you.

> Center yourself and bring to mind your life's journey thus far. Contemplate how every single moment shaped you to be the person you are right now.

102. IT'S NOT PERSONAL.

Learning to not take things personally is a lesson I work on every day. Isn't it interesting how someone's actions or words can cause us to go down the rabbit hole of questioning if what we said or did was wrong? In these moments, we slip into low self-esteem, thinking we are the cause of something that had nothing to do with us. When this happens, let us find the self-confidence to know that we are the only ones responsible for our happiness. We are responsible for ourselves, and others are responsible for themselves.

> Close your eyes and bring to mind a time when you thought someone's mood or actions had to do with you. As you breathe, rise into the realization that it's not personal.

103. YOU KNOW WHAT IS NEEDED.

When you are faced with a big decision and have a gut feeling about what needs to be done, that's your intuition. As a mindfulness teacher, my practices are backed by science. But there isn't hard science to back that deep inner knowing that has no explanation. Once, I was looking to move, and I found a cute apartment online that didn't have the exact address listed. While on a walk with a friend, something told me to turn down a random street, and sure enough, I ended up walking right into the exact apartment. Our soul knows; our intuition is real. Listen to it.

Bring to mind a decision you need to make. Rather than thinking it through, listen to your intuition. What does it say?

104. THE GIFT OF PATIENCE IN LIFE.

When life gets overwhelming, it's easy to become consumed or obsessed with wanting to figure things out in that very moment. When I find myself stuck in the moment, I rest in the present and look to nature for the lesson in patience. Grass grows slowly, flowers blossom in their own time, a tree begins as a seed and over decades grows into a giant, wondrous tree. I have to remind myself that our lives are like this tree. It takes time to grow into something big. It takes time to live; it takes time to exist. This is the beauty of life.

Walk outside and find a tree. As you look up at the tree, contemplate how it started as a tiny seed. Imagine yourself as the tree.

105. TRUST IN LIFE.

Trust in life is necessary, especially when we lose sight of what we think is our path and the next steps are not clear. We must take the risk and trust in the next step we make. I find myself having to surrender to not knowing when making decisions in life. When it comes to my career, I've found that when I make decisions with no secure answer, but follow the feelings of my heart, what is in alignment almost always shows up. Drop down into the heart and trust that it will guide you.

May I trust in life. May I trust that my heart is wise and that life is always working for my highest good.

106. BE FULLY PRESENT.

Fully open up to your experience. See the magic of the present moment. Eckhart Tolle, a teacher and author, often speaks about how the present moment is truly better than any drug out there. When on long silent meditation retreats, we practice mindful walking, an activity that humans tend to rush through. When on retreat, we walk and eat with our full attention. When we walk, we feel the ground beneath our feet as we take each step slowly. With each step we repeat silently in the mind, *I've arrived, I'm home*. With mindful walking there is no destination to which we are headed. Each step is the destination.

Today, choose to walk mindfully. Give it your full attention, and don't rush. Walk slowly, and feel your feet on the ground. Notice how being fully present changes your experience.

107. LET JOY FIND YOU.

Joy can be found in the most unexpected things and ways. This reminds me of a time I went to the farmers' market with a friend. We walked up to a table piled with loose green beans. We looked at the table and looked at each other and burst out laughing. A woman walked by and came up to the table of beans and started laughing with us. No one could explain why we thought the beans were funny, but the fact that it made me, my friend, and the woman all laugh for no reason at all shows us that joy is always there. Joy finds us in our most intimate moments, and reminds us of her importance.

As you move through your day, notice when joy finds you. Perhaps it's in a piece of music, a smile of a stranger, or a table of green beans.

108. IT'S WORTH THE WAIT.

Why is it that humans look for instant gratification? Patience truly is a virtue, and, yes, usually good things are worth the wait. But there's this desire that burns at the bottom of my heart to want to know things right away. Especially in love, I find myself having a hard time waiting. Someone piques my interest, and my heart and mind want to know that person deeply right away. But love isn't something to be rushed; each moment is to be savored along the way. It is the same with life; let us savor each moment as it unfolds.

Close your eyes and sense where you are rushing. As you breathe, sense the beauty in the waiting, trusting the divine timing of things.

109. ALLOW THIS MOMENT TO BE ENOUGH.

This moment is enough. It's hard for us to come to this realization. It's craving, desire, and complaining that pull us away from the present, always wishing for the moment to be different. But what really keeps us grounded in the present is knowing that the moment is enough. In fact, it's more than enough. Even a simple wish for the weather to be warmer or cooler pulls us away from the now. Let us take in the moment as it is and rejoice in what is here, even if it is not what we prefer. Soften into the enough-ness and feel the beauty.

> Close your eyes and repeat silently, "May I accept this moment exactly as it is. May I realize that this moment is more than enough."

110. WHAT KEEPS US SMALL.

Let us not shrink for fear of offending another. Let us say how we feel and express our needs. I'm a recovering chronic people pleaser—a girl who always used to try and be well liked, say the right thing, and take action in ways that people would approve of. But this playing small not only harms us, but also those we try to please, because we are not being honest with ourselves or others. Some of the best advice I learned while building my business is that I must not play small; I must not be afraid of shining too brightly.

> Center yourself and as you breathe, notice where in your life you are playing small. With each breath, allow yourself to shine your brightest light.

111. LOVE IS FLUID.

Love is a way of being; it's omnipresent and transcends all. It is inside of us, outside of us, and all around us. Love is a lot like water: fluid, moving, and always changing form. Love is always present, but we don't always realize it. We suffer when deciding who is worthy of our love, or who will give us theirs, but loving isn't about a giving or taking. We suffer when we try to define what love should look or feel like. The secret is to resist trying to understand love and instead tap into the inner knowledge that is flowing through everything.

> Close your eyes and imagine love as water. Love as raindrops, streams, rivers, oceans, and tears. Feel love's fluid nature within you.

112. LET LIFE MEET YOU.

We are constantly running on the hamster wheel, trying to meet life, or trying to catch up with it. I've found the secret is allowing life to meet me where I'm at. I'm not describing complacency or stagnation, but rather honoring yourself and where you are on your journey and letting life meet you there. Our journeys aren't linear or predictable, and this is what makes the rat race so exhausting. We think we're supposed to be somewhere by a certain time in our lives, and to have accomplished certain things. We're beautifully unpredictable when we create our own unique journeys; let us be open to whatever comes.

> Close your eyes and as you breathe, feel the energy of life meeting you. Sense your body, feel the breath, and notice the sound. Life is here.

113. IT'S NOT ALWAYS EASY, BUT IT'S ALWAYS WORTH IT.

No one said life would be easy. This is a phrase we hear often, and as we grow older we find it to be true. Life is tough, and difficulties are inevitable. But they say diamonds are created under pressure. When life was toughest on me, I learned the most about myself and the woman I wanted to become. When life squeezes us, makes us uncomfortable, and causes us pain, we're forced to adapt, innovate, or change. We're forced to learn about what truly matters to us, the world, and who we want to be. It's not easy, but it's worth it.

Center yourself and notice where life is squeezing you. Notice where you feel you're about to break. Know that this is where you grow.

114. LEARN TO TRUST YOURSELF.

Why is it that we tend to always ask the opinions of others before speaking or acting? Perhaps we fear making a fool of ourselves or displeasing others. Let us learn to trust ourselves, our own judgment, and our own wisdom. Oftentimes when we take the advice of another over our own and it doesn't go well, we are left resenting the other person. If we can learn to surrender to the wisdom of our own hearts, the more authentically our lives will unfold. We can see each moment as a teacher guiding us closer to who we are supposed to become. Every step is our own.

Close your eyes and notice where you seek opinions or advice from others. As you breathe, begin to trust your heart. It will show you the way.

115. LOVE IS TO BE EXPERIENCED.

I'm one of those people who loves to read about love, learn about love, talk about love, and think about love. But sometimes I get so caught up in the reading, learning, and talking about it that I forget to experience it. As humans, we tend to get excited about love, or become curious as to how to heal heartbreak. We seek more clarity or insight into "figuring out" love. But love isn't something to be understood or analyzed; it's to be experienced. No book, podcast, or movie can describe the feelings in our hearts. Love wants to be felt, so feel it.

> Close your eyes and as you breathe, bring to mind something or someone you love. Notice what love feels like in the body and the heart.

116. TRUST IN YOUR UNFOLDING.

Every moment, we are unfolding into who we really are. Just as a flower starts as a seed, a river starts as a drop of water, or a butterfly starts as a caterpillar, we humans are constantly unfolding into our truth. I always imagine my life as a piece of paper folded up with information about who I am and about my life. Each moment that paper unfolds, the more of my life and who I am is revealed. This is the joy of being human—not knowing what you'll discover next. Trust in your unfolding and embrace the discovery of who you are.

> Close your eyes and imagine yourself as a piece of paper unfolding, realizing you know so much, and still have more to learn.

117. MEET YOURSELF WHERE YOU ARE IN LIFE.

I remember before teacher Baba Ram Dass passed away. He spoke of the importance of meeting yourself where you are. He spoke of his life before being a spiritual teacher; then the phase of his life when he was the famous spiritual teacher; and finally the current phase of his life, as an old man in a wheelchair. He said that if he compared his present-moment self in the wheelchair—a time when people helped him go to the bathroom—to any other phase of his life, he would deeply suffer. In order to suffer less, we must meet ourselves where we are.

Center yourself and notice if the mind is pulling you toward the future or past. As you breathe, soften into where you are.

118. WE ARE BORN AGAIN IN EACH MOMENT.

I used to identify with the anxiety that arose in me. I used to identify with being the girl who lost her mother. I used to identify with being adopted. I would take these things on as who I was as a person, as if these labels and experiences dictated my identity forever. Meditation taught me to drop all those ideas, to realize the freedom each new moment brings. Each moment we are truly born again. This idea of being born again is the key to freedom. A label, circumstance, or moment in the past does not determine who we are in the present.

Close your eyes and with each breath, feel that you are being born again. As you breathe, let go of a label you previously identified with.

119. WHEN THINKING GETS IN THE WAY OF LIVING.

Before we make a decision, we tend to weigh the options. We sift out how the moment could unfold. In this hesitation we hold ourselves back. I'm not saying we should only act impulsively, because sometimes that's not good! But we put ourselves through so much unnecessary worry and stress when we over-think. When we overthink or worry, it's almost making ourselves live through the moment twice. A moment hasn't happened yet, yet we think about it, we stress, then the moment actually happens and we live it all over again. Set yourself free from this prison and don't suffer twice. Instead, allow for spontaneity!

Just for today may I let go of overthinking, distractions, and worries. Just for today may I live my life with some spontaneity.

120. WE ARE MADE OF MANY ENERGIES.

We are happy, we are sad, we are joyful, we are angry, we are excited, we are bored, we are loving. Every human has the capac-ity for every feeling and emotion, but so often we choose to identify with one. I always begin my meditation classes by check-ing in with everyone about the emotions they are feeling in that moment. I start every class in that way because every day is a different story. Every day is a new day, and we never know what we're going to get. But that's the beauty of being human; we're like a mixed bag of emotions, never knowing what we'll pull out.

Center yourself and notice what energies are inside of you. What emotions are here in this moment? What emotions stay and what emotions go?

121. THE NEED TO BE BUSY.

In today's society we often equate busyness with success. Success looks different for everyone. For some, success might be based upon the amount they accomplish, while to others success might be how present they were for each moment. Let us reflect on what success means to us. Do we fill our days with activities and tasks to be busy for the sake of being busy? Not to say that a busy day is a bad one, but with my new definition of success, I realize it is less important to fill my schedule and more important to fill my heart.

> Close your eyes and sense the energy of being busy. How does it make you feel? Claustrophobic? Powerful? Urgent? As you breathe, soften and let go.

122. GETTING LOST IN THE STRUGGLES OF OTHERS.

Humans are mirrors. When another is in pain, we begin to see the pain in us. There is beauty in compassion, but when we are listening to friends, we must be careful not to make another's struggles about us. We must be careful to not take on another's pain unless it is ours to take on. I find myself doing both, being quick to jump in with advice. This doesn't help me or the other person. Compassion is the quivering of the heart in the light of suffering. We can feel another's pain, and it opens our heart to be present.

> Close your eyes and sense the struggle of another person that you are carrying. As you breathe, let it go, knowing that you are setting yourself free.

123. LET GO OF WHAT ISN'T MEANT FOR US.

There's that famous saying, "you can't fit a square peg in a round hole." This is true in life as well. I find myself trying to force things that perhaps the universe knows aren't meant for me. I try to force a person to love me the way I think love should be. I try to have control over every aspect of my career. As I grow older, I'm learning to accept that some things just aren't meant to be. The universe has a way of trying to show us what is or isn't meant for us; we just have to listen.

> Close your eyes and see if there's an area of your life you are trying to force. As you breathe, let things fall into place.

124. SEE THINGS CLEARLY.

I always describe meditation as a "clear seeing." Without mindful attention, we tend to look though a foggy lens. With meditation, we shed away the judgments and opinions, and begin to see things as they actually are. I still struggle with always trying to prove that I'm right, or that I know what's best in a situation. But this wisdom of clear seeing reminds me that my view isn't the only view. In fact, my view is clouded with my opinions, judgments, the way I was raised, and many other things. We must step back and begin to see things clearly, as they actually are.

> Close your eyes and imagine your mind as a lens. As you breathe, imagine each breath wiping your lens clean. Open your eyes to the moment.

125. LIFE ISN'T ALWAYS FAIR.

When my mom passed, I would look at my friends with mothers and think life was unfair. I used to think how unlucky I was to have my mother die at such a young age. When we resist reality, we suffer, and it's not productive in your growth or healing. Let us accept reality as it is and surrender in order to move forward. In the moment we may think life isn't fair, or that life is fair, or that we are lucky or unlucky. But life cannot be categorized into those words. Life is life.

> Center yourself and sense where you feel life is "unfair." As you breathe, create space around that label. Can you see it as just life?

126. IT'S ALL ABOUT PERSPECTIVE.

There are so many ways to view things, people, situations, and the world. I've learned there will always be many perspectives to something that may seem very one-sided, clear, or obvious. Our perspective has the power to change our experience. My dad is much older, and I used to constantly worry about losing him. When I shifted my perspective to realizing how lucky I was to have such a wise teacher in my life, I worried less. When we shift our perspective, we're not lying to ourselves, but rather reframing a current situation. We are seeing things in a new light.

> Go outside and look up at the sky. Meditate on how the sky looks different depending on your vantage point, but it is still the same sky for everyone.

127. THE CENTER OF OUR BEING.

When we bring our awareness to the center of our being, we are connected to our Oneness. So much wisdom lives at the center our being, yet we humans spend so much time and attention focused on what's outside of us. I'm guilty of this, too. When I feel unloved, I look for another to love me. When I feel unworthy, I look for someone to validate me. When I feel like I'm lacking, I look for something to fill me up. It's as if there was a void in my center I was trying to fill. But I always come back to knowing that I'm already full.

Close your eyes and allow your awareness to land in the center of your being. As you breathe, feel the fullness inside of you.

128. THINKING VERSUS FEELING.

The beauty of being human is being able to think and feel. I sometimes forget that these two human miracles are different. Love has been my greatest teacher, reminding me that to think about love and to feel it are completely different experiences. Sometimes we get caught up in ideas of what love is supposed to look like. We think about how people should show up in our lives to show us love, and how we should show up. But the problem with getting lost in the thinking is that it pulls us away from feeling love in the present moment.

Close your eyes and notice your thoughts around love in your life right now. As you breathe, feel the love present within you.

129. BE DIRECT.

We always complain about people not being real. But we have no one to blame but ourselves. We live in a world where we mask our difficult emotions to show that we're happy, or buy things when we feel that we're lacking, or look to others for love and validation of our worth. We shouldn't hesitate about being direct if what we want back is realness. I, too, am guilty of feeling something but being too afraid to share it. Let us make a promise to ourselves to show up in the world in a way we would like to see others show up for us.

Center yourself and sense if there is a feeling you are holding back. As you breathe, allow yourself to feel your true being.

130. THE ONLY WAY BEYOND IS THROUGH.

When we experience difficulties, we just want to get them over with. No one wants to be stuck in a moment of stress that turns into an anxiety attack, or a moment of sadness that turns into a bout of depression. But the moment we try to "get over" something is the moment we pull ourselves out of the present, and avoid the feelings that need to be felt. If we truly want to "get over" something, we must be present with it and allow it to teach us what it needs to teach us. The only way beyond is through. Don't be afraid to work through your feelings or ask for help when needed.

Close your eyes and notice what in your life you're trying to "get over." As you breathe, work your way through whatever is arising.

131. WE ARE WALKING CONTRADICTIONS.

Every human is a walking contradiction. This is the harsh but true reality. We identify with labels. "I am a meditation teacher." "I am kind." "I am a daughter." And we feel we must uphold ourselves to the standards that these labels create, but the moment we say or act outside of these standards, we suffer. That is why we should all learn to accept that we are walking contradictions. Yes, it is a harsh reality, but it is also beautiful. It gives us the freedom to be human. I'm a meditation teacher, but I also sometimes get road rage. I am human, a walking contradiction.

Close your eyes and notice the labels with which you identify. As you breathe, allow yourself to be more than the label. You are allowed to contradict yourself.

132. DON'T BE AFRAID OF GROWING.

Humans love to stay in what is comfortable and safe. But oftentimes the danger of staying in what is comfortable is the lack of growth. Sometimes what we need most is a leap toward the unknown, for in this leap we begin to grow and transform. A flower bud blossoming into a flower knows this uncomfortable feeling well. But the flower bud doesn't hesitate—it just blooms. Be like the flower bud and bloom anyway. If we don't, the pain of not growing becomes more painful than the growing itself. Take the leap and don't be afraid to grow.

Center yourself and notice what scares you about growing. As you breathe, imagine yourself like the flower bud blossoming fearlessly into the unknown.

133. YOU DON'T NEED APPROVAL FROM ANYONE.

This is a lesson I'm still learning today. Every successful entrepreneur I've ever met has said this piece of advice will set you free. Don't let the approval of another be your motivation for doing anything. If our intention is to please another, we limit our happiness to the opinion of another and we are bound to be let down. Let your own heart's desire be the fuel that feeds your fire. Our words or actions need no explanation or justification. What we do, say, and who we are needs no permission but your very own.

> May I realize that I don't need approval. May I say what I say and do what I do without explanation. I am me and that is my power.

134. CLINGING.

We humans cling to what feels good. We cling to love, joy, excitement, and silliness because we don't want to let go of what feels good. But the danger of clinging is that it hurts too much when something leaves us. I am guilty of clinging to love, as are many humans. When we feel seen, heard, understood, and cherished by another being, we don't want it to end. But there is so much wisdom in the saying, "if you love something, let it go." There is freedom in knowing that something has come to you because it was meant for you rather than because you fought to keep it.

> Close your eyes and sense what feels good. Notice if you are clinging. As you breathe, let what feels good gently land in your presence.

135. CONNECTION WITH ANOTHER.

We must take time to appreciate our true friends. Friendship is one of the greatest blessings of being alive. Friends remind us that we don't have to journey alone in this world. They remind us that love is possible even when we feel unlovable. They are a second set of eyes and ears, and a second heart when we doubt our own. True friendship is a place where we can feel free to be ourselves without judgment. True friendship is a refuge. Let us meet each other with a friendliness and know that we are making the world a better place.

Center yourself and bring to mind a true friend. Sense how this friendship makes you feel. As you breathe, sense the thankfulness you have for this friend.

136. THE BEAUTY OF ALLOWING.

Even though we know love cannot be forced, it is still something we subconsciously do. We need to learn the beauty and necessity of simply allowing. Rather than changing to be the person we think another wants us to become, we should attract others by being ourselves. When we allow ourselves to be who we really are, that is the most seductive trait of all. Flowers don't go out searching for bees; instead they blossom just as they are, and the bee comes willingly to land on its petals. It is the same with our hearts. Be yourself and allow love to find you.

Close your eyes and pick a quality that you love about yourself. As you breathe, know that this quality is your sweetest nectar. Allow love to find you.

137. YOU'RE ALLOWED TO CHANGE.

How often do we hear our friends say, "you're not yourself today," or "you've changed so much." Know that these phrases are not bad, but rather signs you are human. A natural part of existence is change; in fact, change is the only constant in life. Our existence creates patterns that others see and sometimes depend upon, but then we break these patterns when we grow and evolve. Let us honor our changing selves. Let us remind those around us that there will always be more to know and love about us. Let us celebrate the one constant in life: change.

Close your eyes and feel who you are in this moment. As you breathe, know that you are changing. May you remember you are allowed to change.

138. THE BEAUTY THAT COMES FROM PAIN.

If a sea star loses an arm, a new one begins to regenerate. New life is born from where it has been cut. I think it's the same for humans; often where we are hurt is where the healing begins. It is from my wounds that wisdom and understanding arises. Let us all begin to notice that perhaps this is what life teaches us; beauty comes from pain. Not all pain is bad. It's just a seed planted for wisdom and healing to grow. Let us view pain as a sea star healing from its cut arm—a place where beauty grows.

Center yourself and feel where there is pain. Just as a sea star regenerates an arm, let your breath show you that beauty is growing where you are hurt.

139. THEY DIDN'T MEAN TO HURT YOU.

There's a saying that "hurt people hurt people." When someone hurts us, very rarely does it have anything to do with us. People hurt others because they are hurting inside. What's needed more than understanding is compassion. Meditation has taught me the importance of compassion. Compassion reminds us of our connection to all. When we feel separate, compassion is what brings us together. Compassion means to suffer together. When another hurts you, don't take it personally; instead, look through the lens of love. Their heart hurts and needs your love and kindness more than anything.

Close your eyes and bring to mind the last time someone hurt you. Rather than thinking about your pain, send love to their pain.

140. BE AWAKE TO LIFE.

What I love most about meditation is that it has allowed me to live awake. Before I found meditation, I was just a person in the matrix, doing what I thought I was supposed to be doing, consumed with menial things, tasks, and people. Meditation didn't change my life; instead, it woke me up. It allowed me to see beyond what I physically was seeing and thinking about. There is more to life than what meets the eye. When we are awake to life, we feel it in the heart and soul. We must wake up to life and live from the heart.

May I live life awake. May I feel all I need to feel. May I know that I am not numb and this is a gift.

141. HONOR YOUR UNIQUENESS.

I used to think that being different was weird and "uncool." My love for horses, my brown skin, and the fact that I was adopted were things that I thought made me unlikeable. But really our differences are what make us the unique and strong individuals we are today. Bow to every unique aspect of yourself. We must honor our uniqueness, for it is our special gift to share with the world.

May I celebrate my uniqueness. May I celebrate my differences. May I see that my uniqueness is what makes me beautiful.

142. MOVE BEYOND YOUR OLD WAYS.

There comes a point in time where our old ways of thinking and being cease to work. We get comfortable and feel safe, and then all of a sudden we're forced to change. Not to say our old ways are bad, but no growth comes from comfort and staying the same. Sometimes we are awake enough to hear the whispers from the universe telling us it's time to change. Other times we don't hear, and the universe takes matters into its own hands, forcing us to change. Let us move beyond our old ways into a new, more awake version of ourselves.

Close your eyes and sense your current way of being. As you breathe, feel yourself working your way through this way of being into something new.

143. SADNESS.

It's okay to be sad. I wish this was something we were taught as kids, but instead we're told to "stop crying," or "don't be sad." We're taught sadness is bad, and that is something we carry into our adult lives. Oftentimes we feel ashamed or afraid to admit that we're feeling unhappy. It's okay to be sad. Sadness is a very natural part of being human. When sadness arises, we should meet it with open arms because it's here to teach us something. Let us not be ashamed to be sad, but rather honor the sadness and meet it with kindness, so that we can work through this emotion with ease.

Close your eyes and allow sadness to arise. Meet sadness with a gentleness and kindness, and invite it in. As you breathe, see what sadness has to say.

144. THINKING OUR WAY THROUGH DOESN'T ALWAYS WORK.

There's a common misconception among many humans that we can think our way through problems. Yes, a math equation can be thought through, but life and love and being human are not equations that can be solved. Our minds cling to the illusion of a certainty or security that can be felt but not thought about. So, what do we do when thinking doesn't work? We drop down from our minds and into our hearts. Instead of thinking our way through, we must feel our way through and trust the wisdom in our hearts.

Center yourself and notice your thoughts. Imagine them as clouds passing by, unconcerned with their contents. Allow your awareness to drop down into the heart and feel.

145. OPEN UP TO THE ONENESS IN ALL.

Before I found meditation, I never fully understood or even gave thought to the concept of Oneness. I never took to heart what it meant to be connected to everything. If fact, even thinking about this connection to all wasn't enough. Meditation allowed me to experience Oneness firsthand. This is the gift of the present moment; it's a doorway to experiencing Oneness. The present moment allows us to experience life as it flows through us. The present moment allows us to connect to the aliveness not only in ourselves, but also the aliveness in all things. Aliveness, presence, and Oneness are all the same.

> Close your eyes and sense your aliveness. Understand that this aliveness is in all. As you breathe, feel your connection to everything. Feel your Oneness.

146. IF IT DOESN'T WORK FOR YOU ANYMORE, LET IT GO.

I wish I learned this lesson earlier in life, for I look back on my life and see how much time I spent holding on to people, jobs, and situations that no longer worked. By holding on, I stunted my growth and evolution. We should learn that the moment something starts feeling bad, or we hear the whispers from the universe telling us to change, we should listen and let go. Esther and Jerry Hicks, famous authors and teachers on manifestation, speak about how we've been given an emotional guidance system, and really all we need to do is follow what feels good.

> Close your eyes and feel your emotions. Sense what doesn't feel good and take that as a hint from the universe to let something go.

147. THERE WILL NEVER BE A "RIGHT" TIME FOR ANYTHING.

I was in Bali when I met a man who said something that I will never forget: "Tomorrow isn't promised." This is something I have to remind myself of constantly. My mother's death was the first time this lesson hit me, but of course like all things, I would forget. Her short and beautiful life was a reminder to live each day to the fullest. To say what you want to say, to love who you will love, to hold nothing back. There will never be a right time for anything. The time is now; it's the only time we have.

Close your eyes and contemplate the gift of today. Is there something you want to do or say? As you breathe, realize that tomorrow isn't promised.

148. COMPASSION FOR ANOTHER.

To look at life through the lens of another being is one of the greatest gifts of being human. Compassion not only teaches us to see life from a different perspective but also to feel as another feels. The loss of my mother was something I went through, and it became something that many of my friends would go through. I never realized that the loss of my mother would not only change my life but also be a gateway of compassion for others to turn to me after their own personal losses.

Close your eyes and bring to mind a time you and another have connected because of a similar situation. Sense this connection. Sense the compassion.

149. KEEP GOING.

We must remember that when the going gets tough, we must keep on keeping on. The moments we feel defeated are the times when we need to push through. When I was young, I was told to never give up, and to fight for what I believed in. This lesson is still important as an adult. When we give up, we submit to the role of the victim, and allow life to happen to us. Instead, we need to take on the role of the vessel and understand that life is happening through us. When life knocks us down, let us get back up, stronger, and wiser.

Close your eyes and notice where in life you feel defeated. With each breath, breathe in humility, strength, and courage, and keep going.

150. EMOTIONAL ROLLER COASTER.

Roller coasters are scary for some and thrilling for others, and it's the same with our emotions. Our emotions are not a slow, steady, easy journey. They're filled with ups, downs, twists, and turns. But let us not resist this roller coaster; let's hop on and enjoy the ride. Let us enjoy the laughter, the heartache, the tears, and the rage. We humans have the capacity for every human emotion. Sometimes we are able to recognize and name emotions, and other times feelings cannot be put into words. Let's feel it all. Let's get on the emotional roller coaster and feel what it's like to be alive.

Center yourself, close your eyes, and feel. Let your emotions come and go as they may. Be with them, breathe with them, go along for the ride.

151. MISTAKES DON'T DEFINE US.

If mistakes defined who we were, what a sad story that would be. We must remember we are more than our mistakes. No one can avoid making mistakes; this is a natural part of being human. We misstep, we accidentally hurt people, and we accidentally hurt ourselves. But we humans are resilient beings. Rather than the mistake defining us, let the comeback define us instead. Let the way we got back up when we fell down be what defines us. For in these moments of getting back up, we reveal our true strength, our character, and who we really are. It's in the getting back up that beauty is born.

May I remember that my mistakes don't define who I am. May I remember that it's the way in which I get back up that shows my heart.

152. LET GO OF THE IDEA OF HOW THINGS SHOULD BE.

In striving for some imaginary, perfect, ideal life, we lose ourselves in the beauty that's right here in front of us. Perfection is a losing battle, for all it's doing is telling us that the perfect moment is not enough. We wait for the perfect partner, the perfect job, the perfect weather, but no such things will be found. Perfection is dangerous, so rather than strive for perfection in some imagined future, let us soften into the beauty of now. If we can truly be present, that's where perfection is found. The perfect moment is when the mind and body come together, present to it all.

Close your eyes and sense where you are reaching for perfection. As you breathe, stop reaching and soften into the here and now. The present is perfect.

153. REALLY LISTENING.

When speaking to another person, practice really listening. Practice really hearing someone and what they have to say without making it about ourselves. When we allow for deep listening, we give someone the space to be fully themselves, to express their wants and needs. But we humans always find a way to weave ourselves into a story that has no place for us. Sometimes what's needed is the silence on our end, to just listen and be present for another. So let us challenge ourselves to be silent when another speaks, to hear them out fully so that we're really listening.

> When you speak to someone today, let your ideas of how you relate to another fall away. Allow yourself to be silent, and practice really listening.

154. VULNERABILITY IS BEAUTIFUL.

It's moments of vulnerability that make me love a person. It's showing another who we are underneath our exterior that draws another closer to us. Vulnerability is beautiful. I wish more people knew this, because to me, vulnerability is a clear path to true love. Vulnerability is a sacred space that's created where we can be fully and truly ourselves without judgment of whether what we're doing, saying, or feeling is wrong or right. Vulnerability is full acceptance of the present moment and who we really are. There is so much beauty when we live in our truth and are accepting of another's truth.

> Let down your guard and live in your truth. Be vulnerable, and let another see you exactly as you are. Do the same for someone else.

155. IT'S OKAY TO MAKE MISTAKES.

Every day we strive for perfection, more success, more love, more peace, and more joy. And in that striving, sometimes we make mistakes, we say the wrong thing, and take a step in the wrong direction. That's okay. We all make mistakes. It's when we don't accept mistakes that we end up suffering more. Let us accept this very natural part of being human so that when we do make mistakes, we're able to learn from them. So that when we make mistakes, we own them and move forward. Let us meet our mistakes with grace and ease. Let us allow our mistakes to make us humble, wise, and aware.

> May I meet my mistakes with grace and ease. May I allow my mistakes to teach me. May I allow for them to be what they are: human.

156. BALANCE.

Equanimity is a beautiful quality cultivated in meditation. It's a cultivation of a balanced heart and balanced mind during the changing seasons of life. Equanimity is often described as a mountain in the midst of changing weather patterns. A mountain that remains strong, steady, and unwavering as the rain pours, the sun shines, and the thunder cracks. We must be like the mountain, awake to the changing seasons of life, but remain steady, strong, and balanced. Equanimity is that sense of "okayness" you feel after receiving bad news. It's an acceptance that life is filled with joy, sorrow, and everything in between.

> Things are as they are. May I accept things just as they are. May I accept the changing seasons of life and remain balanced and steady.

157. PAIN AS OUR TEACHER.

There's a reason disease is spelled the way it is. It literally means dis-ease. There's a reason disease manifests in the human body through physical and emotional pain. It's a sign something isn't working, and that something needs to change. Due to my spiritual nature, my mother's stage 4 pancreatic cancer was a clear sign to me that her way of life wasn't working. My mother, a strong, opinionated, kind, and compassionate woman, who was also quite the worrier. I am convinced that her cancer was trying to teach her to let go of control and worry less. When pain arises, let us listen.

> Close your eyes and sense any physical or emotional pain in your being. As you breathe, listen to what it has to say. What needs to change?

158. BE GENTLE WITH YOURSELF.

Be gentle with yourself. We need this reminder daily, because especially in today's world, we tend to be so hard on ourselves. We need to make ourselves our own best friend rather than our own enemy. So, when you are sad, be gentle. When you are mad, be gentle. When you are anxious, be gentle. When you are overwhelmed, be gentle. This gentleness is the kindest gift you can give yourself, for this being human is hard. When we can be mean, let us be kind. When we can be harsh, let us be gentle.

> Close your eyes and notice where you're being hard on yourself. As you breathe, soften and meet yourself with a kind and gentle quality of attention.

159. GENEROSITY.

To give without expecting in return, to hug another for no reason at all, to call a friend just because—are all acts of pure kindness and generosity. Generosity is the antidote for selfishness and hate. Let us help others when they are in need, but let us also help others just from the pure kindness in our hearts. When the world seems cruel, and we lose faith in humanity, it is generosity that brings us back. It is generosity that reminds us that humans can be kind, and that our hearts are filled with love.

Center yourself and bring to mind the last time someone was kind to you for no reason. Rest in what that feels like. Let generosity heal your heart.

160. FILL YOUR HEART WITH WHAT YOU LOVE.

Find what fills your heart with joy and do more of it. Any time I feel down, I do things that bring me joy. I read, I run, I hike, I order in from my favorite restaurants. For it is in this doing that I remember love is also in the being. It is in doing what we love that we seamlessly are able to become love. So, do what fills your heart with love and watch yourself become love. Let your actions remind you of your true nature. Let your actions be a mirror reflecting back the love that is in your heart.

Do something you love and then close your eyes and feel the love in your heart. Imagine love overflowing and touching every cell in your body.

161. ACCEPT THE CHANGING NATURE OF LIFE.

Many wise teachers describe life as changing seasons. Just as spring flowers are bright and blossoming and the winter is cold, our lives, too, weather the seasons. We have moments in life overflowing with joy and happiness, and moments so dark we wish to forget them. This is life. One of my favorite teachers, Jack Kornfield, describes happiness being found when the heart is able to soften and accept the changing seasons of life, whatever they may be. So, let our hearts soften into the now, exactly as it is, and invite it in with love. From this place of acceptance, true love is possible.

> Center yourself and feel the current season of life, all the thoughts and feelings. As you breathe, soften and invite in this moment as it is.

162. LOVING ANOTHER BEING.

I think the reason so many are obsessed with love, finding love, or being in love is because it is something close to pure ecstasy. A feeling of being both lost and found at the same time. To be loved and chosen by another, accepted for who you are, cherished, respected, and worshiped. I myself am a hopeless romantic, but sometimes to a fault, seeking it out where it isn't. I think true love and all its lessons reminds me that loving another being is a reflection of the way you love yourself. Love yourself the way that you want to be loved.

> Close your eyes and meditate on what love means to you. As you breathe, love yourself the way you want another to love you.

163. STAY OPEN.

In a world where it's so easy to become closed off, let us challenge ourselves to stay open—to love, to change, to possibility, to the truth. Being open with yourself and others is a gift. When we remain closed off, there's no room for anything. Sometimes I close myself off for fear of getting hurt, but all I'm doing when I close up is hiding myself from the truth. When we close ourselves off, it's like a horse wearing blinders; we are only able to see straight ahead, missing all the possibilities for beauty that surround us.

> Center yourself and, with your eyes open, allow for a soft gaze on everything that surrounds you. As you breathe, allow your heart to open.

164. THE RISK OF LOVING.

The risk of loving is something I feel in my heart every day. I hold back, thinking I'm protecting my heart, but the protection is just an added layer and barricade that love needs to penetrate. So the risk of loving fully and without hesitation is something I am trying to do. Can we all show up in love and life in this way, putting ourselves and our hearts out on the line, risking being hurt or rejected all in the name of love? Why do we wait for the conditions to be safe, certain, or perfect? Let us risk loving now.

> May I take the risk of loving. May I risk showing my heart and my true feelings. May I do it all in the name of love.

165. WE THINK WE KNOW.

Our human minds love to know. Our minds love to solve problems and figure things out. If something feels out of place, the mind tries to think itself to peace. Once the mind thinks it knows, the universe shows us we really can't know anything but the present moment. We think we know a person. We think we know how a situation will work out. We think we know where we belong. If meditation has taught me anything, it's that I know nothing at all. And in this, there is freedom.

Center yourself and bring to mind something you think you know is certain. As you breathe, begin to contemplate that you don't really know anything.

166. WHATEVER ARISES.

Be open to whatever arises. Whatever thoughts, feelings, and sensations come, let them be. Before I found meditation, I used to block out anything that didn't feel good, like an emotion that was heavy or a thought that was stressful. But I've learned that in order for things to fall away, they first must come up. So, invite in whatever the present moment brings. Let it arise, be with it gently, and let it fall away. We must continually fill and empty our hearts to make room for our truth of who we are becoming in each moment. So, whatever arises, let it.

Close your eyes and allow your awareness to rest in the heart. Feel the heart as different emotions rise and fall. Let it flow.

167. THE OPINIONS OF OTHERS.

We tend to look through a narrow lens of our own views, opinions, and understanding. Let us widen our lens and take into account the opinions of others. Let us leave room for another's reality, and listen and learn. We must understand that no two people are the same, and that is beautiful. Let us widen our lens and widen our hearts. For in this widening, we create a spaciousness and room for others to be, express themselves, and share their hearts. Let us share ideas and perspectives, and live in an open and accepting world where love can grow.

Center yourself and bring to mind an opinion another has shared with you. Can you listen without judgment? Can you make space for another's reality?

168. AFTER THE PAIN.

Just like after the rain there are flowers, after the pain there is growth. It's like airing out a wound. A wound needs air to heal, and our pain needs time to heal. But after pain there is growth, and after a wound there is a scar. And in that scar, there is healing and wisdom from what hurt us and forced us to grow. So, we must trust the pain, trust the time, and trust what will come after. We must carry our scars and not our wounds. We must wear our scars as our greatest accessory. There is wisdom after the pain.

Close your eyes and feel your pain. As you breathe, know that after the pain there is beauty. From the wound there will be a scar of love.

169. WE ARE ALWAYS GUIDED.

We are always guided. I know this to be true because the sun always rises and sets. There is an unspeakable force guiding every being here on this planet; we just need to look for the signs. After I lost my mom, I kept seeing monarch butterflies around me. I knew instantly in my heart that those butterflies were her. After I nailed a job interview, cried from heartbreak, or was walking peacefully in nature, a monarch butterfly would always flutter by, letting me know she was guiding me.

Close your eyes and feel the unspeakable force of life that guides you. How does it communicate with you? Through nature? Animals? The sun?

170. EVERY MOMENT IS A TEACHER.

Our life and our journey are a never-ending lesson. Every moment is a teacher. But what is this lifelong lesson we're here to learn? I believe the lesson is truth. In each moment we are peeling away layers of ourselves to find out more about who we really are. We get to know people on a deeper level to truly see their soul. We experience hardships and difficulties to know our strength and resilience. We fall in and out of love to know what the heart is capable of. Every moment teaches us the lesson of truth and life.

Center yourself and sit quietly. What is this moment trying to teach you? What are you learning about yourself? What are you learning about the world?

171. ATTENTION.

Why do we humans equate success with fame, power, and attention? If we do something notable, why do we desire another person's validation to be seen and heard? This is something I contemplate often, as I find myself wanting to show the world my accomplishments and receive recognition for them. This isn't a bad thing, but I think as humans, we should become mindful of our intention behind attention. Our journey to success is a lonely one if we constantly seek approval. But it doesn't have to be lonely if we ourselves give our journey our own attention and learn to celebrate ourselves.

> Close your eyes and give attention to yourself and this moment. Celebrate your favorite aspect of you in this moment. Give attention to your existence.

172. BE SELFISH WITH YOUR WELL-BEING.

The best advice I ever got from my friend and fellow teacher was to be selfish with my well-being. With that piece of advice, I got better at saying no, I got better at expressing my boundaries, and I got better at knowing who I am and valuing my worth. We should all learn to be selfish with our well-being, because it makes us show up in the world as better individuals. If we are constantly giving ourselves to the world to the point of breaking, what good will that do? Be selfish with your well-being, put your happiness first, and from there you can fill others.

> May I learn to be selfish with my well-being. May I understand happiness is my birthright. May I make my well-being a priority.

173. OUR PAST CAN BE HEALING.

The roots of trees aren't as pretty as the leaves and are often hidden away, but they are necessary for the plant to exist. The same reasoning goes with our past. Our past is necessary for us to grow into the people we are today. No, our past isn't always beautiful, but it was a necessary part of our growth and healing. Let us view our past as the roots of a tree that allows our leaves to grow, and is essential for our becoming. Our past can be healing; we learn from our past to show up wiser in the present.

> Go outside and look at a tree. Look down at its roots. They're sometimes hidden, sometimes visible, but always there. And a necessary part of that tree's growth.

174. A WISH FOR YOUR OWN HAPPINESS.

Happiness is our birthright. We must not forget this. In meditation there is a practice known as loving-kindness. It is a well-wishing for our own happiness and the happiness of another being. The Buddha said that if our practice doesn't include ourselves, it is incomplete. So, let us start with wishing for our own happiness. Let us recognize that this is not selfish but selfless. Let us be happy so our being can show others that happiness is their birthright, too. We should do what makes us smile daily, and savor that feeling. Happiness is something we should feel often.

> May I be happy. May I be peaceful. May I be well in mind and body. May I feel safe and protected. May I feel loved and worthy.

175. LITTLE JOYS WAITING TO BE FOUND.

Little joys are all around us, reminding us of the possibilities for happiness that are here in the present. I always talk about joy and have my students pick something small, something that isn't obvious. Little joys, such as how the sun warms my face, or the sound of birds as I walk to my car, remind me of the thrill of being alive. For it's the little joys that we take for granted, and sometimes miss completely. So, let us open our eyes, our ears, and our hearts to the little joys that are everywhere.

Walk outside and close your eyes. Listen to sounds. Feel the sun and the wind. Joy is here. Joy was waiting for you.

176. WE ARE MORE THAN ENOUGH.

Oftentimes we are stuck in a trance of unworthiness. We strive for perfection, more love, more success, more peace, more joy, and so on. We fear that we are not good enough. This, my friend, is an illusion. You are more than enough. You were born enough, and you will always be enough. You are YOU, and this is a gift to the earth. The earth is lucky to get to experience your uniqueness. You are perfectly imperfect, so bow to that. It is your greatest gift, and you are worthy of it all.

Sit quietly, close your eyes, and sense where you feel you are lacking. As you breathe, slowly remember that you were always enough and will always be enough.

177. ACCEPTING WHO WE ARE AND WHO WE ARE NOT.

Often we identify with how we are feeling in the moment. "I am angry." "I am successful." "I am a failure." But we must remember the beautiful gift of discernment. To also take into account all that we aren't. We are constantly changing, peeling away layers of ourselves as each moment passes. So, I think it is unwise to overidentify with any thought or feeling that arises in the moment. Artists create a masterpiece from nothing. What starts as a blank canvas, or a chunk of stone, is slowly painted or carved away to reveal all that is from what was not.

Close your eyes and feel all that you are. As you breathe, feel all that you are not. Feel that you are everything and also nothing.

178. THE DANGERS OF IGNORANCE.

Some say ignorance is bliss. Sometimes this may be the case, but ignorance is a denial of what is true. It is willfully looking away. So, may we have the courage to face the truth even if it means the truth is painful? Let us have the courage to be truthful in our being. May we have the courage to face the harsh truths of the world. For the moment we give up ignorance, we open ourselves up to the beauty that also lives in truth. The truth can scare us and disappoint us, but it can also teach us and heal us.

May I no longer hide from what I know is true. May I no longer turn away in fear. May I have the courage to face the truth.

179. OPENING TO WHAT IS TRUE.

Opening to what is true takes courage. For many humans, we choose to stay closed for protection, for fear that the truth might hurt us. Let us have the courage to open up to what is true. Yes, sometimes this might mean making a big decision like leaving a partner whom our soul knows is not right for us, or leaving a job we've been at for years because it is not our heart's calling. This might even be something small like having the courage to get up and out of bed and show up in the world as best we can in the moment.

> Close your eyes and sense a decision you are trying to make. As you breathe, feel the courage in you to open up to what is true.

180. THE DANGERS OF SEEKING APPROVAL.

Why do we humans seek approval and so desperately have the need to be right? Something spirituality has taught me is that someone who has a different view than me isn't wrong. Rather, they are just looking at life through their own lens. So, I try to challenge myself and contemplate the intentions behind my words or actions. Do I do and say things because I want someone to think I'm right? Or am I just living out the truth in my heart?

Let us act in a way that is not to gain approval or prove our rightness.

> Center yourself and notice the intentions behind your words and actions today. Make it your intention to express your heart's truth.

181. RISING AND FALLING.

When I first started experiencing anxiety attacks, I used to say "my anxiety." When I would speak with friends about mental health, we all used language such as "my depression," or "my sadness." But when we used words such as "my," we chose to call it our own and identify with these emotions as part of who we are. This is dangerous. I had a teacher once tell me, "Laurasia, how selfish of you to say anxiety is yours; it is an emotion that rises and falls in everyone." His words changed my life forever, and now it is a lesson I teach my students.

> Close your eyes and notice what emotions you are currently experiencing. Rather than saying "my," change your language to "_____ is arising." You are not alone in this feeling.

182. LOVE WHERE YOU ARE.

Let us all learn to love where we are. We humans are so goal-driven; we keep our eyes on the prize. And we forget to enjoy the journey along the way. Let us remember to love the ground upon which we stand now while being driven. I'm not saying give up and let go of our goals, but rather let us fall in love with where we are on our journey, too. There is so much beauty in each step. Let us love the process. Let us love our unfolding. Let us love the unveiling of who we are in each moment.

> May I fall in love with where I am, and remain excited about where I am headed. Let me love the journey and what I learn along the way.

183. ACCEPTANCE LEADS TO CHANGE.

Many of us turn to meditation looking for change—to change our previously stressed, controlling, numbing ways. But we must not meditate looking for change. Instead, meditation requires an open and accepting heart to whatever is true about ourselves and the world in the moment. Change can occur from that place of acceptance. For so long I didn't want to accept that I was feeling anxious or depressed, and I did everything I could to deny myself of that truth. Meditation made me look anxiety and depression in the eye, acknowledge and accept that it was there, meet it with kindness, and then it began to transform.

> Close your eyes and sense what is true about you in the moment. As you breathe, rather than trying to change, soften and allow it to be.

184. PATIENCE WITH OTHERS.

We must learn to be patient with others. Of course it is very natural to want another human to act a certain way or say a certain thing, but we must remember we cannot control others. This is a lesson I'm reminded of often, especially in love. I've found that I suffer when I expect someone to show up in a certain way. I want them to text or call or spend time with me in the way that I want, and on my timeline. But the world doesn't work like that. Love doesn't work like that. Patience is needed. Waiting is a beautiful thing.

> Center yourself and sense how the urgency for another to show up in a certain way feels. With each breath, invite in patience.

185. BEYOND WORDS.

The words "I love you" and the feeling of love hit differently. When I think of love, it's the feeling that courses through my veins that teaches me what love is, which is more powerful than the words of love ringing in my ears. Let us experience a life beyond words. Let us soften into the feeling of being alive. Let our experience be what we remember most rather than the spoken words and the empty promises. Life is about the moments and how they felt, rather than the words and what they meant.

Meditate on the words "I love you." Then meditate on the feeling of love itself. Notice how the words sound and how the feelings feel.

186. FEAR AND LOVE.

There is only fear and love, and our lives flow between the two. We either act or speak out of love or fear. Think of that fear as just a wave in the ocean of love. The next time you speak or act, notice if it is coming from a place of fear or love. Just as the wave is a part of the ocean, fear will come and go and dissolve into love. We must remember that waves are turbulent and can cause damage like a tsunami. But it is the ocean that holds it all. It is the ocean that is vast and wise.

Close your eyes and feel how there is both love and fear in your heart. Imagine the fear as a wave in the ocean of love.

187. THE GIFT OF BOUNDARIES.

I never truly understood the gift of boundaries until I became an adult. I used to think someone telling me no or setting limitations was harsh. But I realize now that boundaries truly are a gift. To know yourself well enough to know when to say no. To know when you've hit your limit. To know when you need to rest. It is through boundaries that you show the world your worth. So, when I encounter someone who sets boundaries, I respect them. I try to honor myself in that way, knowing my own worth and standing in my power.

Close your eyes and sense your worth. What boundaries do you need to put into place so that others will know your worth, too?

188. THE KINDNESS OF ANOTHER BEING.

When a person is kind to me, I remember it in my heart. It is as if my heart has been touched by their heart. I remember when my mother was sick with cancer and how my friends showed me kindness. These acts of kindness and friendship are something I will never forget. And so, in a world where it is easy to be cruel, I try to always be kind. I do this so the person does not lose faith in the world or humanity; instead the person is reminded that there is still good in the world.

Close your eyes and recall a time someone was kind to you. Recall the feelings that arose knowing that someone cared. Savor the kindness of another being.

189. DON'T CHANGE TO PLEASE ANOTHER.

This one seems obvious, but I find myself in this predicament more often than I'd like to admit. When I get excited about love, I find myself changing into what I think the person wants to see without even realizing it. But if we feel we need to change, then it isn't love. To me, love is a place where we allow another to be perfectly themselves without trying to fit them into our idea of some perfect image. Let us make a promise to be ourselves and trust that the right people will be drawn to us and love us as we are.

Recall a time you have changed for love, or a time you expected someone to change for you. Let ourselves and others be as they are.

190. AGITATION.

I used to think being agitated was a bad thing, but now I see this as a moment to learn. Mindfulness has allowed me to view agitation as an emotional teacher. Agitation can cause us to act out in anger, sadness, or disassociation because it makes us feel uncomfortable. But rather than avoiding what is uncomfortable or acting out against it, let us soften into discomfort. Let us become curious as to what these agitations are trying to teach us. Let us allow these ripples in the water to settle so we can see what rests underneath.

Close your eyes and see what is causing an agitation in your heart. As you breathe, allow the heart to soften and see what there is to learn.

191. TRUE UNDERSTANDING OF ANOTHER.

To understand another deeply is true connection. Several years after losing my mom, I befriended a girl in my boxing class who lost her mom shortly after we met. Having both been through a similar struggle made our friendship stronger, knowing we both experienced similar feelings of loss, grief, and heartbreak. We both had to move on with our lives without the presence of a mother. To truly understand another adds a layer of love that makes us feel seen and heard.

Close your eyes and think of someone in your life who truly understands you. Sense this connection and how it feels in your heart.

192. THE HEALING POWER OF CONNECTION.

Human connection is one of the greatest healers. Human touch is the greatest medicine. Sometimes I forget this, and I get on a streak of thinking that I'm independent and don't need anyone. And while, yes, being independent is good, too, we tend to forget the necessity of human connection. Connection and touch remind us that we are not alone in life. As Christopher McCandless wrote in *Into the Wild*, "Happiness is only real when shared." So please don't stop being a strong and independent person, but also invite in the magic and healing that connection to another being can bring.

Meditate with a loved one. Sit together in silence and feel each other's presence. Feel the unspoken connection that heals you both. End this meditation with a hug.

193. TRUST THAT PEACE IS YOUR NATURAL STATE OF BEING.

Just like a snow globe is clear after the snow settles, underneath all our daily struggles and suffering is peace. Our minds are very much like a snow globe. Our heads get clouded with thoughts and feelings that pull us away from our natural peaceful state of being. But we must remember that peace is our true nature, so that when we do get shaken up like a snow globe, we know that the snow of our struggles won't last forever. Knowing that peace is your natural state of being keeps hope alive. Peace is your natural state of being.

Close your eyes and recall the last time you were upset, but then smiled or burst out laughing. Remember that moment as proof that you are peaceful.

194. YOU ARE NOT YOUR WOUNDS. YOU ARE YOUR SCARS.

We always have a choice. We can identify with our wounds, or we can learn from them. We can learn from the moments that broke us down and wear our scars proudly. When we learn to decipher the difference between a wound and a scar, we find freedom. When we see the beauty in a scar, we fully acknowledge the wound and what we went through without being limited by it. We see that the scar carries elements of the wound but also the lessons we learned from the pain as well as the wisdom we gained from healing.

Center yourself and feel what you have learned from your struggles. The past is the past; don't let it limit you. Let what you've learned carry you.

195. THE COURAGE TO BE WHO YOU ARE.

Love lives in each of our hearts, even if we can't feel it. But once we become aware of this love, all we want to do is find someone worthy enough of receiving it. It's like a little fire burning inside the heart, wanting so desperately to be felt. I find myself in moments of feeling this fire but too afraid to show it, fearing that showing too much of myself and what the heart actually wants will scare someone away. I'm still learning that with the right person, the love in my heart won't scare anyone away.

> Close your eyes and feel the flame of love burning in your heart. Have you been holding it back? Have the courage to be yourself fully.

196. IT'S OKAY TO NOT HAVE ANSWERS.

It's okay to not have answers yet. We humans are always in a rush to have answers now, to solve problems and figure things out as fast as we can. But we must remember there is a beauty in the waiting. There is a beauty in the question. For humans, things seem so urgent, but really, what's the rush? All we have is time, and the beautiful present moment, to be savored and embraced. Let us let go of needing to know anything right now and soften into the question. Let us embrace the moment without answers yet.

> Close your eyes and sense the spaces between each breath. See the beauty and wisdom in the spaces. Let go of any urgency within you right now.

197. STRUGGLES MAKE US STRONGER.

When I think of moments of struggle being worth the fight, I think of salmon swimming upstream. This is what they do. When life gets hard, we have to struggle. But struggling doesn't always mean fighting or powering through. Sometimes the strength from our struggle comes in the letting go. Trusting that when we jump we'll be caught, or when we stop swimming we'll float. Let us not look at struggling as sometimes bad, but instead as a stepping stone that gets us to where we need to go. It's the struggles that make us stronger.

Close your eyes and recall a struggle in the past that made you stronger. Sense how the moment of struggle taught you to trust.

198. THE FEAR OF GETTING HURT IS A RISK WE MUST TAKE.

In order to feel love fully, we must risk showing all of our heart. Like a baby bird learning to fly, we must take the risk and leave the nest. We must leave what we know as safe, secure, and protected in order to fully feel love. We must trust that in showing ourselves fully, we will be shown what we need to see. We might be shown rejection, or we might be shown love. But it is the risk we must take so we don't go wasting more time in the empty promises of those who do not know where our heart lies.

Close your eyes and sense where in your heart you've been holding back your love. As you breathe, allow your heart to open and show itself.

199. WE ARE ALL HERE FOR A REASON.

It took my mother's passing, the most tragic event of my life, for me to find my path. The moment I started listening to my heart's calling and following what gave me joy, I started to believe that truly every person here on earth has a purpose. My mother's death led me to spirituality; specifically, it led me to meditation. Meditation offered me the peace and kindness that I had no idea I needed. Every day, my students remind me that I am living out my life's purpose. I know in my heart and soul I was put here to teach.

Close your eyes and allow your awareness to land in your heart. What is your heart's calling? What is your reason for being?

200. ACCEPTING WHAT IS.

We must come to terms with the moment in order to grow. This is a lesson I learned after my mother's death. Too often I see people stuck in the past, wishing that things turned out differently. But if we get stuck in the trap of trying to change what cannot be changed, we leave no room for growth. We must accept what is, even if the present moment is hard to accept. Acceptance is an understanding of what is. Acceptance of what it is to be human. Acceptance of what it is to live life, however beautiful, and however tough. Let acceptance set you free.

May I accept the present moment as it is. May I understand that the past is gone and that the future is not yet here.

201. TAKE A BREAK FROM TRYING TO FIGURE EVERYTHING OUT.

Sometimes we just need to give our minds a break, and rest in stillness and silence. Sometimes trying to solve all our problems and answer questions becomes too much. The world and our problems become too heavy to hold. So, let us give ourselves rest when it's needed. Our problems can wait; they'll be there when we come back. Give your thinking mind some time off. Walk outside in nature, close your eyes, listen to sounds, smell the world, feel your feelings. Let the mind take a break and rest.

Go outside and as you breathe, unhook from the thinking mind. Feel your feet on the ground, sense your body, sense your breath, feel your heartbeat.

202. DARKNESS AND LIGHT.

The world is full of both darkness and light, the yin and yang. This is what makes our existence so dynamic and so beautiful. The sun rises in the daytime, and as it sets, we see the light of the moon shining in the darkness. Flowers open and close, humans wake up and then go to sleep. We are happy, then we are angry. Life is hard, then it feels effortless. Life is a constant push and pull of the light and the dark. Let us embrace this beautiful juxtaposition we call life.

Go outside and watch the sunset. Watch as light turns to dark. Watch as the moon shines her light in the darkness. Experience the darkness and the light.

203. BE BRAVE.

We must be brave, for being human isn't for the faint of heart.
We will be tossed and thrown every which way; our hearts
stretched so thin they break. Life is tough, this we know, but
we must be courageous. Be brave so you can be reminded of
your resilience, so you can be shown your sensitivity and your
strength. Show the world you can get back up. No mountain
too high, no lake too wide. You will make it through. Be brave
to show others they can do it, too. Life doesn't throw at you
what you can't handle.

Close your eyes and promise yourself you will show up
to life with an open and willing heart. Promise yourself
that today you will be brave.

204. FIND COMFORT IN THE DISCOMFORT.

Life gets uncomfortable. Our challenge as humans is to find
comfort in the discomfort, for this is what will get us through
life's toughest moments. To find comfort in the uncertainty,
and to make peace with the unknown—this is the secret to
living. For when we soften into the unknown and get comfort-
able in the feelings that make our skin crawl, we learn the most
about ourselves. I once heard a Buddhist monk say meditation
didn't heal him; it made him a connoisseur of his neurosis.
This is the gift of meditation; it gives us the tools to work with
the unworkable.

Center yourself and allow your awareness to rest in what
feels uncomfortable. As you breathe, allow the area
around the discomfort to soften.

205. WE CAN HOLD IT ALL.

Our hearts are as wide as the ocean. Really, they're wider, but I think the ocean perfectly captures what I'm about to describe. Emotions, thoughts, feelings, and sensations—they're like waves, and they have the power to really disrupt our well-being. Waves can cause storms, they can cause ships to sink, they can cover a city in a tsunami. But fear not, because our hearts are wise and vast, and they can hold it all. We humans can handle it all. Sometimes it might not seem like it, when we feel like we're about to break, or like we cannot continue on. But we always do.

> Close your eyes and feel the entirety of being human. Notice all your thoughts, feelings, and sensations. As you breathe, trust that you can hold it all.

206. LIFE TEACHES US HUMILITY.

We embarrass ourselves. We make mistakes; we stumble and fall. It took me years to truly know what it meant to live humbly. Too often I would try to show off, or act like I knew more than whoever I was talking to. But as I grow older, the more I realize that I knew nothing. And so, to live humbly is to carry myself in a way I've always been, but always learning more. Taking risks, getting hurt, standing back up. Making a fool of myself, laughing at myself, and carrying on. Let us live humbly and laugh our way home.

> Close your eyes and recall the last time you made a fool of yourself. As you breathe, laugh at yourself, for in the laughter is wisdom.

207. LOOK BEYOND OUR DIFFERENCES.

We are drawn to people with similar views, opinions, and outlooks on life. But this natural human tendency to surround yourself with what seems familiar is so limiting. Some of my closest friends are very different from me. These differences have allowed me to look at life in a new way, and see certain situations with a new perspective. What I'm realizing is that when I think I know something in its entirety, there is so much more to know. There are many different ways to see things, and always new lenses to look through.

Close your eyes and recall a time when you thought your way of viewing things was the only way. As you breathe, widen your view.

208. PLAYING IT SAFE.

When it comes to physical safety, I think, yes, play it safe. Guard this vessel that is our body. But when it comes to matters of the heart and love, don't play it safe. People would advise me to guard my heart so I wouldn't get hurt. And yes, to some this might be their approach to love. But for me with matters of the heart, I'm learning that the heart wants what it wants, and when we don't honor it, we suffer. So, when it comes to the heart, don't play it safe. The risk of loving will be worth it.

Center yourself and sense the love in your heart. Imagine it like a flame burning bright, a flame that cannot be contained. Let it burn.

209. DIFFICULTIES ARE A PART OF LIFE.

Imagine a flower bud becoming a flower. It is already the flower before it blossoms. We must remember to appreciate the bud and what it's becoming. It is the same with our difficulties. Difficulties are a part of our becoming; they are what make up the bud and they are what allow it to blossom. It's like our difficulties are the rain and our joy is the sun; the bud needs both in order to grow. Once we can accept this fact of life, we can appreciate the difficulties and understand that it is just part of the process of becoming who we are.

Close your eyes and imagine yourself as a flower bud. Rather than focusing on becoming the blossomed flower, allow the rain and difficulties.

210. SOME THINGS WE MUST DO ALONE.

Of course it's nice having someone with us to experience life, but some things must be done alone. This is a realization I've had on my journey of self-love. So often we seek love from another, but first we must find it within ourselves. We must raise our own vibration in order to call in someone who matches that vibration. I used to look for the love in another to fill a void, but really that void could only be filled with the love from my own heart. Notice what you are seeking and look within.

Center yourself and as you breathe, sense your courage. Know that you have what it takes. Everything you are seeking lives inside your own heart.

211. RIPENING INTO WHO WE ARE.

In each moment we are becoming more ourselves. But we must be careful to not judge our insides based on our outsides. I've found myself in this predicament quite a few times, being a generally happy person who smiles a lot. I'm able to teach a class about joy and happiness with a smile on my face and a lightness in my energy, while secretly my heart aches. It's like a fruit that looks ripe on the outside, but then we bite into it only to find that the fruit is spoiled or underripe.

> Close your eyes and sense your body and your emotions. As you breathe, feel the soul that lives inside your body. Be okay with the difference.

212. RESTLESSNESS AND UNCERTAINTY.

Restlessness is so common. So, when it arises, do not fret. The inability to find stillness and peace in an ever-changing world is also part of this human experience. When restlessness arises, do not try and force stillness. Instead, honor your inability to be still. Bow to the restlessness; perhaps it's trying to teach you something. Whenever restlessness arises for me, I view it as a lesson in needing to accept the uncertainty of life, of a situation, of a relationship, of literally anything that I need to know. Honor your inability to grasp that which cannot be grasped.

> Close your eyes and sense any restlessness. Rather than trying to will it away, invite it in. Let it work its way through your body.

213. GROWTH AND TRANSFORMATION.

Out with the old and in with the new. There is so much wisdom in this old saying. Part of growth and transformation is all that no longer serves you will fall away. Old habits, thoughts, and even the people and situations in your life begin to fall away as you become more fully yourself. As you evolve, your environment begins to match your vibration. As we grow, our physical bodies literally begin to change—as a flower grows and its petals fall off, a snake sheds its skin, or a baby chick hatches out of an egg. This is all a part of the process, so honor it.

> May I honor my growth and transformation. May I allow what no longer serves me to fall away, and invite in all that adds to my evolution.

214. INTIMACY AND PLEASURE.

Intimacy and pleasure are basic human needs but are perhaps not talked about enough because they are taboo topics. We need intimacy and pleasure to survive, so let us invite it in when it finds us. Let us not be ashamed of experiencing bliss through the connection of another being. Let us not be ashamed of experiencing bliss by ourselves. Intimacy to me is a closeness, and pleasure is joy experienced through the body. So, let us put down our walls, allow ourselves to be completely revealed, and open up to the pleasure in the present moment.

> Close your eyes and as you breathe, put down your walls, allowing the feelings of bliss in the mind and body to find you. Savor it.

215. BE LIKE A RIVER.

Let us be like a river—fluid, venturing to uncharted territories, and leaving parts of itself behind. We humans are fluid; in every moment we reach new parts of ourselves and the world that we have not yet explored. We are like the water flowing through the river, which carries parts of itself while leaving the rest behind. Sometimes when feelings rest too long inside of us, they become poison. They consume us and our minds and hearts without us even realizing it. So, let us learn to be like the river; be okay with changing and leaving parts of ourselves behind.

Close your eyes and imagine yourself as a river. Notice any feelings that have been resting inside you for too long. As you breathe, leave them behind.

216. SURRENDER.

Every time we fall asleep, we surrender to the universe, trusting we will awaken the next morning. I've learned that there is so much wisdom in surrendering, trusting that what needs to happen will happen. We create so much of our suffering trying to control everyone and everything around us. We create this false sense of urgency in our minds that things need to be figured out right now. What's needed is more surrender and trust. We must focus on the art of allowing, trusting that things will fall into place as they should. Each time we fall asleep we practice this art.

Before going to sleep, notice this trust you place in the universe that you will wake up the next morning. As you drift off, allow yourself to surrender.

217. SOFTEN INTO LIFE'S CHANGING NATURE.

Life is always changing. Time is passing us by; the seasons are changing, and we are getting older. As the earth spins, the cells in our bodies die. This is the law of the universe. It's when we are at odds with this universal law that we begin to suffer. We try to hold on to our youth. We try to hold on to people. We try to hold on to the parts of the world that are meant to move. When we resist life's changing nature, we interfere with the way of the world. Let us soften into life's changing nature and allow life to flow through us.

May I accept life's changing nature. May I soften into life's natural flow. May I understand that change is a part of life.

218. BY CHANCE.

As I grow older, I am learning that nothing happens by chance, but that there are divine inner workings behind everyone and everything. I've become less of a believer in coincidences and a full believer in alignment with the universe. I've had so many experiences and met so many people who were supposed to be in my life. Once we awaken to the synchronicities of life, then we can begin to view even the most difficult moments as lessons. Being human is a miracle; let us wake up to it. Life isn't happening to us; it's happening for us. Let us wake up to this miracle.

Close your eyes and realize that you are a miracle. As you breathe, understand that nothing happens by chance. Life is happening for you.

219. RESISTING CHANGE.

When things change inside of us, things change around us. It's like pruning a plant. Sometimes the old leaves or petals fall away, and sometimes you need to go in and prune the ones that are dying. It's the same with our lives. As I grow older and become wiser, I notice my inner world changes along with my outer world. And this change is okay. It only makes sense that the people or situations that I outgrow no longer align with me or my vibration. Let us invite in this change, let our old petals fall away, and let us be okay with outgrowing things.

Close your eyes and as you breathe, allow the old parts of you and your life to fall away. Allow your outer world to meet your inner world.

220. LIVE OUT LOUD.

Let us live without hesitation, let us boldly be ourselves, and let us live out loud. I've come to realize that holding back any part of myself does me no good in the long run. We cannot let things fester, for they will manifest in our bodies and lives in some way, shape, or form. So, when you want to say something, say it! If you feel a feeling bubbling up inside of you, let it feel its way through. On days when I feel trapped in my head, I turn on some music and dance like no one's watching. I feel better every time.

Close your eyes and sense what your soul wants in this moment. Without hesitation, do it! Let your soul sing and express itself.

221. WE HAVE ALL SURVIVED SOMETHING.

We are all survivors of life. No matter what we have gone through, this is the invisible thread that connects us all. I remember feeling so alone when I first started experiencing anxiety and depression. But when I began meditation, I realized these feelings are experienced by all humans in some way or another. As I began teaching and sharing stories of these emotions and how they affected my life, all my students would nod their heads. These moments make me realize that we're all survivors together. We're all doing the best we can; we're all going through it together.

Close your eyes and sense whatever struggle you are currently facing. As you breathe, sense that you are not alone. We are all survivors.

222. LEAN INTO THE VASTNESS OF YOUR HEART.

When we can't hang on any longer, let the heart hold you. We try so hard to love and be loved, to be seen and heard and appreciated for who we really are. It's exhausting. Sometimes people let us down, sometimes situations disappoint us, and sometimes things go entirely wrong. So, when we feel like we can't hang on any longer, let us fall into the vastness of our hearts, and let our hearts hold us. I remember moments of deep sadness after the loss of my mother and after breakups. I felt like I could not continue on. My heart took the lead when I couldn't.

Center yourself, and just for a moment stop trying to hold on to anything. Let yourself sink into the vastness of your heart. It's got you.

223. ASK FOR HELP.

When we feel isolated and in need, let us turn to the help of another. Let your guard down; let your vulnerability and softness show. I used to think asking for help was a sign of weakness. But as I grow older, I'm realizing asking for help is a sign of strength. In asking for help we admit to our humanness. We admit that, yes, life is tough, and sometimes we need to lean into the connection and aid of another. It sometimes takes more courage than we could imagine to admit we need help, and even more courage to actually ask.

> Close your eyes and sense the courage in you to ask for help when you need it. Sense the strength in knowing someone can help.

224. WHAT YOU ARE, NOT WHAT YOU KNOW.

I used to think what I knew defined who I was, but I realize now this is far from the truth. Deep human connection is formed when we let go of all we think we know and show up truthfully, honestly, and humbly. Human connection is formed by being who we are. When we're able to let go of our need to prove our worth by what we know, and show our worth by simply being, we are living in our truth. Let us live by who we are and not what we know.

> Close your eyes and let go of all you think you know. As you breathe, show up truthfully and humbly. Show your authentic self.

225. WHEN WE DON'T GET WHAT WE WANT.

Disappointment is unavoidable. When we don't get what we want, we tend to react in anger or sadness. Over time I've learned that the way I choose to respond to disappointment completely changes my experience. Rather than responding with resistance, let us respond with ease. This is not to say be happy when things don't go our way, but instead let us understand that this is a part of life. I remember going through breakups, fighting to keep a relationship in place that wasn't meant to be, and in that fighting I suffered. The moment I accepted the breakup, I began to heal.

> Recall the last time something didn't go your way. How did you respond? The next time something doesn't go your way, respond instead of reacting.

226. THE PAST IS GONE. THE FUTURE IS NOT YET HERE.

Every time I find myself stressing out about love and life, I always reread Eckhart Tolle's *The Power of Now*. It's times when I feel dysregulated, anxious, and depressed that I have to remind myself of the present moment. The present moment has a way of putting an anxious or depressed mind at ease. In the present moment there is no reaching or ruminating. I've suffered in reaching for the perfect future or found myself stuck in memories of moments that have passed. I must remind myself the past is gone, and the future is not yet here. All we have is the present.

> Close your eyes and allow your memories of the past and your worries of the future to fall away. Sense yourself in the present.

227. FEELING DEEPLY IS A GIFT.

To feel deeply is a gift. It's a sign we're alive; a sign we're not
numb. Modern medicine has created medication to numb, as
if feeling deeply is a sickness. Of course we humans love to
feel happiness or excitement. But when anxiety or depression
or rage arise, we run for the hills. This is only accepting half of
life, the yin without the yang, the light without the dark. Let us
learn to accept all of life and its feelings and invite in the full
texture of life. Let us feel deeply and know that we are alive.

Close your eyes and recall a time you were the happiest
and the saddest. Allow the two moments to fuse together
in your being.

228. DOING AND BEING.

There is a difference in what we do and how we exist. The
Western world puts value on doing more. Busyness is seen
as a sign of success. The practice of meditation is sitting in
stillness, resting in nondoing, and just being. We get to know
ourselves better in stillness. Doing sometimes is a distraction
to our soul, pulling us away from what our souls want to say.
Let us find the beauty in not doing anything at all. Let us rest
in the magic of being and listen to the soul speak.

Close your eyes and sit in stillness. Let go of the need to
do anything and rest in your being. Simply exist breath
to breath, moment to moment.

229. LIFE IS AN INITIATION.

The first time I heard that life is an initiation was in mind-fulness teacher Jack Kornfield's book *After the Ecstasy, the Laundry*. Life truly is an initiation, and every moment truly is a teacher. Our proudest moments teach us as well as our dark-est moments. Each moment is an unveiling of who we really are and what life is really about. I love Jack Kornfield's take: "There are no enlightened beings, only enlightened moments." That statement allowed me to soften into my humanness. It allowed me to accept the moments that felt far from spiritual as lessons, too.

Close your eyes and as you breathe, sense that this moment is teaching you something even if you can't see it yet. Trust in life.

230. RIGHT WHERE YOU'RE SUPPOSED TO BE.

Wherever we are on our journey of life, know that we're always right where we're supposed to be. We're only "lost" or "off track" if we are headed somewhere in particular. We tend to get so fixated on destinations, on what we think our path is supposed to look like, or we get stuck comparing our path to another's. But the truth is that there isn't a "correct path"; there is no timeline to our becoming. Over time I've learned to trust each moment, however difficult, however joyful, knowing that's where I was supposed to be.

Center yourself and let go of any destination on which you are fixated. As you breathe, trust that where you are is where you're supposed to be.

231. EVOLVING UNCONSCIOUSLY.

We're always healing and evolving whether we realize it or not. If you had asked me during my darkest days if I knew that I was going through deep healing, I would have laughed. But in hindsight, when I look back at my life, it's the moments of great struggle and suffering that my greatest healings have taken place. So, let us not forget that even if we can't tell we're healing, we actually are. The days when I feel extra anxious or depressed, I have to remind myself that even those moments are moments of growth.

Close your eyes and soften into the moment. Know that in this moment you are healing and growing, even if you can't feel it.

232. AN ENDLESS UNCOVERING.

Life is an endless uncovering of who we truly are. Each moment we learn something new about ourselves. As we move through life, we feel as if we've finally gotten to know ourselves, then another veil is lifted: a new emotion, a new clinging, a new aversion. But do not be discouraged; this endless journey is what makes our lives spiritual. We get to know our soul better in every moment, and just when we think we know it, we learn more. We are like onions with many layers to peel away, getting to know ourselves deeper with each breath we take.

Close your eyes and as you breathe, imagine each breath uncovering a layer of who you are. With each breath, you are getting to know yourself better.

233. THE DAILY ACT OF LOVING OURSELVES.

Empty promises lead to broken hearts. Over time, I've learned that when someone says they love you or they promise you the world, they don't mean it. It's not in the words that love is found, but in the actions, in presence. I'm learning to take people's words on love lightly and wait to see how they show up in love by their way of being. When someone fully embodies love, romantically or not, you can sense it in their presence. When someone walks, talks, and breathes love, you can tell. It's not something I can put into words, just something that needs to be felt.

Close your eyes, breathe with love, listen with love, sit with love. Let love radiate from your heart and into every cell in your body.

234. WALLS BUILT AROUND THE HEART.

We build walls around our hearts. We try to keep out the fear of the future, a painful memory of the past, or even the risk of deep love. But rather than keeping out what we don't think we want in our heart, perhaps these feelings are trapped inside. In fact, what these feelings need is to be felt so that they can make their way out. So, let us be careful to not build walls around the heart; we never know what we're trapping inside or keeping out. Let the heart be open and ready to feel what it needs to feel in order to be free.

Close your eyes and sense the walls you've built around the heart. Notice what you have been trying to keep out. As you breathe, open your heart.

235. A LIFE BEYOND LABELS.

We are quick to name feelings and label them "happy," "angry," and "sad." But the deeper I dive into spiritual practice, the harder it is for me to label them, for I just go from feeling deeply to lightly and my life flows between the two. I've found that naming my emotions does nothing to make them feel any stronger or any less. When I don't try to name feelings and I remain in the present, it's freeing because the feeling can be what it is without me trying to put it in a box and label it and remedy it.

> Close your eyes and let your feelings be what they are, without trying to diagnose or remedy them. Let these feelings be nameless.

236. OUR AWARENESS IS VAST.

Mindfulness is an evidence-based awareness practice where we pay attention on purpose to the present moment. There is an element of spirit, source, and mysticism that I cannot put into words, and can only be experienced through practice. There's a part of our awareness that understands the magic of the universe, that knows that we are guided. I believe meditation is magic. In the beginning, all skeptics thought it was something esoteric, but these practices are now also backed by science. Meditation hardwires happiness into our brains, thanks to neuroplasticity. The recipe for happiness is a little bit of meditation and a little bit of magic.

> Close your eyes and allow your awareness to remain open, taking in the reality of the moment as well as the magic. Your awareness is vast.

237. HONORING ANXIETY.

I used to run from the anxiety that arose in me. It wasn't until I started meditating that I realized anxiety is one of my greatest teachers. Instead of running from anxiety, what I needed to do was turn toward it and honor it. Anxiety is the natural human reaction to worrying about the future. Amit Ray said, "If you want to conquer the anxiety of life, live in the moment, live in the breath." Anytime anxiety arises, it's the mind traveling to the future in fear. Let us remember to come back to the present moment and come back to the breath.

Close your eyes and notice your mind's tendency to visit the future. As you breathe, come back to the moment, the here and now.

238. FEAR PREVENTS CLARITY.

Fear has a way of preventing us from seeing clearly. Fear makes us blind. Being human, we will always have fear, but knowing how to remove its blinders is key. Fear clouds us from seeing the present moment. We fear what the future holds, we fear feelings, we fear the unknown. Not to say that we should never think about the future, but we must visit the future lightly and with discernment, accepting the uncertain nature of the future. Let us not be crippled and blinded by fear. Let us remove our blinders and begin to see clearly.

Center yourself and sense any fear that is present. Notice how it blinds you. As you breathe, begin to see beyond the fear. See the present moment.

239. BELIEVE IN YOURSELF.

Imposter syndrome is a natural human reaction to start-
ing something new. As I write this book, I realize that I'm an
author. Before I wrote this book, if someone had asked me if
I was a writer, I would have said no. The thing about life that
I'm realizing is that we become what we already are. I'm the
author before I start writing, I'm the meditator before I sit
down to meditate. We are in a constant state of becoming; it's
silly to limit ourselves and say we are something once we've
achieved it, because it limits our potential. Let us embody who
we are and what we are becoming.

Close your eyes and sense what you aspire to be. As you
breathe, know that you are already what you want to be.

240. SEPARATION AND BELONGING.

We humans waver between separation and belonging. At
moments we feel we are unique individuals with unique prob-
lems that no one can understand but us. We feel we must seek
validation and possessions from our outer world. We define
success as buying more things and making more money. Some
moments we feel connected to all beings, sensing the Oneness,
that we belong to something greater than ourselves. We then
define success as a happiness we find inside ourselves. The
genuine shared wish among all humans is to be happy. We feel
we are separate, and we feel that we belong.

Close your eyes and sense your separateness and your
connectedness. Allow yourself to flow between being a
unique individual and belonging to a greater whole.

241. IT ALL BEGINS WITH AN IDEA.

Everything starts as an idea. We plant the seed, and then we watch the manifestation grow. The seed we plant is an intention, an idea that guides us on our journey. The beauty of setting intentions is that we become aware that we are guided. It becomes very clear what is or is not in alignment with our idea. Once I learned about setting intentions and manifestations, I realized I truly was the author of my life. Meditation taught me to set intentions such as "May I be kind to myself today" and "May I meet this difficulty with compassion." When I worked with these intentions, my life became those things.

Close your eyes and set your intention to call this into your life. Visualize your intention, feel how you want to feel, and embody it.

242. BEING SELF-CONSCIOUS.

For many years of my life I would speak and act in ways to please others, for fear that everyone was always watching me and judging me. But living in this way made me feel like a bird trapped in a cage. I was always self-conscious and afraid to be me. People are judgmental and will continue to be. But knowing that judgment tends to be a projection of someone else's insecurity within themselves has allowed me to stop taking judgments personally, and has given me the courage to be me. We must uncage ourselves to set our hearts free, so we can live life freely and dance like no one's watching.

Close your eyes and recall the last time you felt self-conscious. Imagine yourself as a bird letting yourself out of your cage and flying free.

243. WHAT GROWS INSIDE US.

When I first began teaching meditation, I used to prepare. I would think of a lesson, write down key points I wanted to speak on, and then teach. But soon after I began to feel more confident in teaching, I realized I didn't need to prepare, because everything I needed to know was already inside me. All the wisdom is already inside all of us; underneath the fears and insecurities is all we need to know.

> May I know that everything I seek is within me. May I know that beyond the fear, doubt, and insecurities lies all the wisdom I'll ever need.

244. OUR INNER-KNOWING.

When we are babies, we all crawl, we learn to walk, and we learn to speak. It is something that comes naturally to all human babies; their inner-knowing leads them to their own evolution, just as every caterpillar knows they must build a chrysalis to become a butterfly. Anytime I feel like I'm losing my way, or find myself confused, I drop down into my heart and trust my inner-knowing. It's like when people tell you to trust your gut. Each of us knows what to do; it's our thinking mind that tries to convince us otherwise.

> Center yourself and bring to mind an issue you are trying to figure out. As you breathe, trust that you know the answer.

245. IN OUR ELEMENT.

Outside of meditating, one of my favorite hobbies is boxing. Ten years ago, I would have never guessed boxing would be for me. I started boxing in my early twenties, and a form of presence and joy came over me. It was a feeling I had never felt before. When I box, I am in my element. Find something that makes you feel in your element, and do it often.

> Close your eyes, and ask yourself, "When is it that I feel most in my element?" Whatever comes to mind, do that, and often.

246. LIFE IS ONE BIG EXPERIMENT.

Life is testing us constantly. I truly believe the universe is here to make sure we live out our authentic purpose. We will be given opportunities to stay on our authentic path, and tests that will try to lead us astray. We should learn to tune into our hearts and notice what people, environments, and situations feel in alignment and which do not, then use that feeling as our guide.

> Close your eyes and imagine life as one big experiment. Each step you take and move you make is a test in life.

247. THE GIFT OF POSSIBILITY.

Difficulties that weigh on our hearts are just like the fog—they roll in and then clear away. On the cloudy days it's possible to forget that the sun is burning bright on the other side of the clouds. When we are in the thick of our difficulties, it's hard to remember happiness and joy are on the other side of the moment. Let us learn to remember the gift of possibility. That even when we are sad, stressed, or full of rage, happiness is still possible. Over time the sun burns away the fog. Our happiness will burn away our pain.

Close your eyes and sense whatever difficulties are currently fogging the heart. As you breathe, remember that happiness and joy are still possible.

248. OUT OF OUR HEADS AND INTO OUR HEARTS.

Why is it that we humans try to experience lives through our minds and not our hearts? I've found that more wisdom comes from feeling and experiencing life, rather than trying to comprehend life and its meaning. Knowing the physics and aerodynamics behind basketball does not guarantee we can play like Kobe Bryant. It is the same with life; the more we know about the science of happiness doesn't make us happier. It is what we do with what we know, and how we feel in the present moment and in our hearts, that allows us to truly be happy.

Close your eyes and as you breathe, get out of the mind and into the heart. Trust the feelings in the heart without trying to analyze them.

249. EXPERIENCE AND UNDERSTANDING.

We humans acquire knowledge in two ways—by learning and then understanding, and by doing and then experiencing. The two ways of learning work together symbiotically. Learning and understanding without action is just information in the mind. Doing and living without awareness and understanding is living mindlessly. So, let us embrace the understanding of life and experience it in our living.

Close your eyes and as you breathe in, take in life as you understand it in this moment. As you breathe out, be with what is.

250. SOMETHING NEW.

We humans tend to stay with what is safe and comfortable until it begins to feel uncomfortable. Then we begin to itch for something new and different. We also tend to fear leaving our comfort zones because what is new is unknown. Meeting what is new with grace and ease takes skill. Without awareness, something new can seem overwhelming and make our minds spin, because we have not yet met what lies ahead. Let us move from the old to the new with awareness and the understanding that what is new is unknown. Let us meet the new and unknown with kindness and curiosity.

Center yourself and sense your comfort zone. Notice how it feels known. As you breathe, find the courage to meet what is new and not yet known.

251. PEOPLE ARE MIRRORS.

I have a friend who truly is my mirror. She's always the one who reminds me of my accomplishments when I seem to completely miss them. She's the one who always points out my strengths and kind heart. She's the one who tells me I'm expansive and wise. But the thing that makes her my mirror is that I tell her back what she tells me. I'm always in awe of her wisdom and grace, congratulating her as she blossoms and grows. The thing is, we both know we are these things, but in those moments when we forget, we're there to show each other our own reflection.

> Bring to mind a person whom you love and admire, who also celebrates your being and existence. Realize that you are reflections of each other and yourself.

252. EYES ARE THE WINDOWS TO THE SOUL.

When we look another in the eyes, we get a sense of their soul. It's not something that can be seen in the eyes, but it's something felt in the heart when the eyes meet. There's a reason the saying "the eyes are the windows to the soul" is so famous; it's because everyone has experienced this truth. The moment we make eye contact, we have a deep understanding of another without exchanging any words. You can feel another's joy and suffering as if it were your own.

> Look someone in the eyes and notice how you feel. Sense what the eyes say without any words. Feel their soul as you gaze into their eyes.

253. WE LIVE, WE LEARN, WE CONTINUE.

We get the same lessons over and over in the form of different situations. We meet the same souls in the form of different people with different masks. We feel the same emotions through different causes and conditions. This is life, a series of repetitions in different forms. Let us not feel disheartened by this fact but instead humbled. As each experience, person, or feeling comes our way, it teaches us. We live it, we learn, and we continue on. Just as the sun rises and sets each night, and the earth spins.

Close your eyes and imagine yourself as the earth spinning slowly as the sun rises and sets. This is you existing in perfect harmony with life.

254. THE BEAUTY IN OUR STORY.

There is beauty in our story, and each time we tell it, we learn more about the world and our hearts. When my mother died, the first time I shared the story of her death, it was a fresh wound that needed airing out to heal. Today, as a meditation teacher and student, I tell the story of her death often, and all the lessons it taught me and continues to teach me over time. This story that used to feel shameful and dark is now my greatest source of light. This is the beauty of our stories—each time we share them, we grow.

May I know that my story is beautiful. May I share it knowing both the teller and the listener have something to learn.

255. WHAT HAS BROUGHT YOU HERE.

Every step you've taken has led you here to this exact moment. The universe led you to pick up this book and read these words. Every heartbreak teaches us what love is and is not. Every moment of loss teaches us what it means to appreciate and when to let go. Every moment of stress teaches us to let go and trust. Every step we take has a purpose, propelling us forward to our soul's calling. So, let us trust each step as we walk into the unknown, knowing that it is leading us to where we are meant to be.

Look down at your feet and as you walk, know that with each step you are arriving. Each step is toward exactly where you are supposed to be.

256. THE RISK OF ACCOMMODATION.

I used to be a chronic people pleaser, always making sure that those around me were happy before tending to my own happiness. But in this accommodation of others' happiness and well-being, I kept parts of myself hidden, for fear of shining too brightly. We lose ourselves in the moments of trying to uplift another. Let us shine brightly, and in that brightness, let it bring to light another's glow. Let our own joy and happiness show another that they are worthy of it, too. Let us not get lost in accommodation or keep any part of ourselves hidden.

May I shine brightly and be who I am. May I no longer lose myself in accommodating others. May I remind others of their own light by shining.

257. WE MUST BELIEVE.

We must believe the universe is always conspiring for our highest good. It's easy for us to believe this when things go our way and we get what we desire. It's during life's tougher moments when we need to trust and believe. One of my favorite manifestation teachers, Lacy Phillips, has a term for when it feels like all bad things are happening: the magic dark. Because it is the magic dark that signifies greatness is coming. I know that when life gets tough, the universe is just preparing me for the magic that's about to unfold. We must believe that life is happening for us.

Close your eyes and as you breathe, know that whatever difficulties you are going through are just clearing the way for the magic that's about to happen.

258. STOP PREPARING TO LIVE. JUST LIVE.

My favorite teacher, Thich Nhat Hanh, always talks about Westerners being so good at preparing to live but not good at actually living. He points out how we will dedicate 15 years to get a diploma, a job, a car, a house, always looking for happiness sometime in the future. We must become aware of the happiness in the present moment. It's hard to do when the norm seems to be preparing to live, but once we wake up to the magic of the present moment, we realize we have no other choice but to live in the now.

Close your eyes and as you breathe, become aware of the present moment. Let go of all plans for the future and be here now.

259. UNCONDITIONAL LOVE.

Unconditional love is a love without judgment, a love that shows up no matter what. I'm still learning to unconditionally love myself and others. Would it really be love if we only loved ourselves on the good days? Would it really be love if we only appreciated some qualities in another and not all of them? Unconditional love means loving myself on the days I find it hard to love myself. It means hugging your friend even when you don't agree with them. It means meeting ourselves and others with compassion, kindness, and nonjudgment, and loving anyway.

> Close your eyes and find a part of yourself that's hard to love right now. As you breathe, love that part of yourself anyway.

260. LIFE IS OUR GREATEST TEACHER.

We are so lucky to be a student of life, the wisest teacher there is. Countless hours spent in the classroom, hundreds of books read, thousands of hours spent on the meditation cushion, and none of that time learning could ever compare to the lessons life has taught me. I have spent much of my life reading and talking about love, but none of this has taught me as much as loving itself. It is the same with life. We can read all the books, take all the classes, learn from all the teachers, but nothing will teach us as much as living life.

> Center yourself and as you breathe, realize you are in life's classroom. Know that whatever you are going through is today's lesson.

261. DIVINE MOMENTS.

Divine moments are those moments that feel like miracles. I experienced one of my life's divine moments when I was on the top of Machu Picchu in Peru. There was a moment shortly after I made it to the top that a monarch butterfly flew past my head. Peru was a place my mom always spoke of wanting to visit, and after she passed I knew it would be the first trip I would take. My mother's spirit always visits in the form of a monarch. That moment of magic meeting reality was proof to me that life is something greater than we perceive it to be.

> Recall a moment that seemed as if you were experiencing magic here on earth. As you breathe, sense the divinity in you and the world.

262. RECURRING LESSONS ARE NOT FAILURE.

Life is full of recurring lessons. Just like the seasons change and waves continuously crash on the shore, lessons are brought into our lives. Thinking of life as a series of repetitions might be disheartening. But it's more like waves crashing on the shore, making the sand smooth each time. We receive each lesson in divine timing, and when we need it. And each time the same lesson appears, we are wiser, kinder, and more understanding. Each time a lesson appears in our lives, there is something new to learn. When we choose to read books again, each time we learn something new.

> Close your eyes and bring to mind a lesson that is recurring in your life. This not a sign of failure, but a moment to learn.

263. SECURITY OR FREEDOM.

Philosopher Alan Watts said, "If, then, we are to be fully human and fully alive and aware, it seems that we must be willing to suffer for our pleasures." In order for us to grow spiritually, we must learn to understand this. I used to live much of my life trying to distract myself from feeling anything too deeply, for fear of getting hurt. But as I've grown spiritually, I've realized each of us is given a choice, to live awake or asleep. We have a choice to stay safe in our illusion of security, or wake up to the freedom of feeling awake to life.

Center yourself and sense if you feel numb or awake to life. As you breathe, ask yourself, "What choice will I make today? Security or freedom?"

264. THE HEART KNOWS BEST.

The heart always knows. It's why we can try to convince ourselves someone loves us but know in our heart that they don't. Or we can tell ourselves that we're happy working countless hours at a job we hate, but the heart feels empty. Why do we humans do this to ourselves? Why do we lie to convince ourselves the heart doesn't feel what it feels? Let us learn from this, come out of our thinking minds, and sink into the wisdom of the heart. Our minds keep us safe, but our hearts keep us true.

Close your eyes and sense a lie your mind is currently telling you. As you breathe, sense the truth that rests in the heart.

265. LET GO OF YOUR PAIN.

Let go of your pain if it weighs heavy on the heart. Letting go of your pain doesn't mean ignoring it or dropping it out of your awareness, but rather understanding that something hurts and then moving forward with your life. Jack Kornfield said letting go is really letting be. Pain only weighs heavy when we cling to the stories around the pain, or resist the fact that something painful happened. It is in this clinging or resistance that pain begins to fester. By acknowledging what happened with understanding, we let it be. We let it go.

Close your eyes and sense any pain you are carrying. As you breathe, acknowledge its presence with kindness and understanding. Then let it go.

266. LEAN IN.

The only way out is in. I used to either avoid my anxiety by numbing or distracting myself. It wasn't until I learned meditation that I realized I no longer ran from the anxiety that arose in me. Instead I leaned in to meet and embrace it. Now, what I'm describing isn't succumbing to the thoughts that accompany anxiety, which ultimately leads to an anxiety attack. Rather, lean into anxiety and meet it for what it is: an emotion that rises and falls in humans. With mindful attention, lean in, get curious, and find your way out.

Center yourself and notice what emotions you've been avoiding. As you breathe, find the courage to lean in, and meet these emotions with kindness and curiosity.

267. FORGIVENESS IN ACTION.

Forgiveness is a daily practice. It is something that is necessary to move though life without being weighed down by all those people who have hurt us. For years I carried anger around my birth mother, for the way she spoke to me after my mother passed, and for the way she speaks to me now. Thich Nhat Hanh said anger is just not fully understanding. I began to realize I didn't fully understand what my birth mother went through. Every day in my meditation practice, I send her forgiveness. I understand I will never know what it's like to live in the Philippines and give your own child to another.

> May I forgive those who have hurt me. May I realize I will never understand the inner world of another being. May I forgive.

268. LIFE IS TO BE LIVED, NOT UNDERSTOOD.

I've spent countless hours reading self-help books and years attending meditation trainings, silent retreats, and classes—all in an attempt to understand life, love, and why I am the way I am. But as I grow spiritually, I'm realizing life is to be lived, not understood. Author Mark Nepo wrote, "If you try to comprehend air before breathing it, you will die." Yes, I've learned about life, love, and the nature of the mind in all the ways previously described, but there is no greater teacher than living, loving, and being me. Sometimes what's needed is to stop overthinking and to start living.

> Close your eyes and begin to breathe. Think about the breath, then just breathe without any thought behind it. Notice the difference. What feels lighter?

269. WE ARE EXTRAORDINARY.

I always used to be self-conscious of my voice. Growing up I hated hearing it, wishing my voice were less annoying. Today, what students and strangers compliment me on the most is my voice, and how it awakens the heart and makes people feel calm. My voice didn't change, but what did change was perspective and my illusion of perfection. I realized my voice is what makes me unique. I stopped viewing my voice as a flaw and began looking at it as something extraordinary. Let us remember we are not perfect. We are extraordinary.

Close your eyes and bring to mind a quality you view as a flaw. As you breathe, realize it is this quality that makes you extraordinary.

270. FLOWING NOT FORCING.

When talking with one of my students about love, she gave me a great piece of advice: Everything we want is downstream. I realized this applies not only to love, but also to life as well. Alan Watts describes life as one giant stream and that we suffer when we try to swim against the stream. I've noticed myself trying to force so much in life—force love, force work, force plans, force people—and let me tell you, very rarely does force work. Let us practice less forcing and more flowing. Let us let go of control, and be with what is.

Close your eyes and notice what you are forcing. As you breathe, be with what is. Allow yourself to flow down the stream of life.

271. PAIN TRANSFORMS INTO WISDOM.

When pain is met with resistance, we suffer; when pain is met with love, we transform. So, love hard on the pain that arises. Love hard on the anger, love hard on the sadness, love hard on the confusion, love hard on the stress—for each of these pains is teaching you about life. The pain of grief that I experienced after my mother died is not something I would wish on anyone, but for me, it was necessary in my awakening. The moment I decided to love the pain instead of run, I realized that the grief was teaching me about life.

Close your eyes and feel any pain weighing on the heart. As you breathe, imagine the breath touching every cell with love, transforming it into wisdom.

272. NUMB OR AWAKE, THE CHOICE IS YOURS.

We can live life numb or awake; the choice of how to live is ultimately up to us. To be numb is to ignore difficulties, suppress emotions, or run from life when it gets hard, and to identify as a victim that life is happening to. To be awake is to be fully present to life, to every emotion, to every sound in the body, and to allow yourself to experience all that a moment has to offer. People choose the numbness thinking it will keep them safe and free from pain. But when we choose to be awake, we see the wisdom that rests in everything.

Close your eyes, and make a choice today: Will you live numb or awake? Will you choose to run from the moment? Or open up to it?

273. ONENESS.

Oneness, spirit, and the universe to me all mean the same thing. It is this indescribable force that connects us all together and to ourselves. Alan Watts describes life as one giant stream that we are all flowing down. This giant stream is Oneness. It's the force of life that connects us all to our own emotions, our experiences, and to one another. It connects every human to one another and to our world. None of us is going through life alone. Oneness reminds us that life is much greater than our own experience of it, and it is in us all.

> Close your eyes and imagine flowing down the stream of life. As you breathe, realize that everything inside of you and outside of you makes this stream.

274. BE LESS CONCERNED WITH WHY, AND MORE CURIOUS ABOUT WHAT.

It's our stories about why things happened to us and our stories behind why we feel the way we do that add an extra layer of suffering. With awareness, we are given space to step back from the stories consuming the mind, and we should become curious about what we're experiencing in the body. It's the why that pulls us away from the present moment into memories of the past or worries of the future. It is the sensations of what is happening in the body in that moment that bring us back to the here and now.

> Close your eyes and sense what emotion you're currently experiencing. Become curious about what this emotion feels like in the body rather than why you're feeling it.

275. BEING AND BECOMING.

When we are fully present, we are being. As we live and care for the present moment, we care for who we are becoming. This lesson hit me when I went skydiving after graduating from college. As I jumped from the plane (with my spotter of course) I remember it felt like I was falling into who I was becoming. The present moment was falling into the future. Life is like skydiving, in that we take the risk of living in the moment while not yet knowing what lies ahead—but knowing that every moment led you to that point.

> Close your eyes and sense yourself existing in this moment. As you breathe, know that you are also becoming who you are meant to be.

276. NO ANSWERS ARE NEEDED.

There are no answers needed yet. Everything is happening exactly as it should. Let us surrender, trust, and allow life to unfold. I need to remind myself of this, especially in love and the direction of my life. I meet someone new with whom I connect, and I find my mind trying to analyze the meaning behind every word and gesture. Or I find myself trying to map out my career path, and how much I want to accomplish and by when. Sometimes I just need to breathe and remember that life is unfolding exactly as it should, in perfect timing.

> Close your eyes and notice what questions arise in life and love. As you breathe, trust in the timing and unfolding of your life.

277. SURVIVING OR THRIVING.

Meditation helped me shift out of surviving and into thriving.
I used to allow the anxiety and depression that would arise in
me to control my mind and ruin my day. Meditation taught me
to lean into those emotions, to own my ugly, and from that
awareness and kindness I began to thrive. Now I teach the
tools of meditation for a living. Sharing with others what used
to ruin my day is the medicine that made me who I am today.
By simply being with and meditating on the emotions that
scared me, I went from surviving to thriving.

Close your eyes and sense what emotions are scaring
you. As you breathe, sense the courage in yourself to
allow these emotions to strengthen you.

278. PASSION.

To me, passion is an expression of presence and joy in doing
something we love for the joy of simply doing it. Growing up
I was a passionate child—passionate about ballet, horseback
riding, and art. As an adult I've learned that passion is more
than the hobbies I love. It's spending time with those I love,
meditation, traveling, going for a hike, seeing the sunrise,
laughing so hard I cry. Passion is the beautiful gift from life
that we feel in our bones. It's the joy of being fully present in
life and love.

May I sense the passion inside of me burning like a flame
inside the heart. May I sense passion filling my heart
with joy and presence.

279. YOUR GIFTS.

We each have unique gifts to offer the world. We find these gifts by being our truest selves. When we discover our gifts, we live our purpose by sharing that love with the world. We share not only by physically teaching another, but also by teaching in our being. When we see another person has tapped into their gift—whether it's singing, writing, playing football, or arguing in a courtroom—we experience the passion and love they have for their gifts, and perhaps we, too, are inspired. Let us tap into our gifts and use them daily. In our way of being, let us inspire others to use their gifts.

Close your eyes and sense what gifts you have to offer the world. What did the universe give you to be a living expression of love?

280. THE PACE OF LIFE.

When I was a child, all I wanted to be was a teen, and as a teen all I wanted to be was an adult. As an adult I find myself wavering between clinging to my youth and wanting to rush into what I want my life to be. The secret to life is in the way we navigate the rushing and the slowing down. Meditation taught me to slow down to the speed of life, while honoring the mind's natural tendency to rush to an imagined future. Let us slow down to the pace of life and be here in the present.

Close your eyes and sense life happening around you. With each breath, slow down to the pace of life. Be with life as it unfolds.

281. EVERYTHING AND NOTHING—IN ANOTHER.

My mom's death taught me more about life than I could ever imagine. In her absence I learned more about who she was and about love than I learned while she was alive. One might think when one is alive that they are everything, and when they are gone, they are nothing. But for me it seems the opposite is true. When my mother passed away, I felt more connected to her spirit and wisdom than ever before. It was when I realized her physical self was no longer that her soul was in everything. I experienced everything in nothing and nothing in everything.

Close your eyes and think of a person you've lost. As you breathe, sense in their absence that nothingness turning into a presence. A presence that is felt in everything.

282. YOU ARE RESILIENT.

Just like waves crashing on a shore and smoothing the rocks, our difficulties remind us we are resilient. It is the same with being human. When we go through the toughest breakup, first we lose hope in love and then we start to feel better. We lose a loved one and experience a grief so deep we can't stop crying, and then we begin to smile in the memory of their presence. We experience an anxiety so intense that we feel like we are going out of control. Then, just as the snow settles in a snow globe, we are clear and calm. Let us remember we are resilient.

May I remember that I am resilient. May I remember that when I fall, however tough, however scary, I am strong and will get back up.

283. VICTIM OR VESSEL.

My friend and meditation teacher, Bryan Ellis, said we can choose to be a victim where it feels like life is happening to us, or we can choose to be a vessel where life is happening through us. I look at my own life and see where the choice to be a vessel changed my life. When my mom passed, I could have easily spiraled into being the victim, dwelling on thoughts of my mom not being able to see my wedding or meet my children. Instead I chose to be a vessel, understanding that her death was my teacher.

> Close your eyes and sense that life is happening through you. Choose to be a vessel today. Understand that life is happening for you.

284. FAILING WITH GRACE.

It's not the fall that defines who we are but the way in which we get back up. Failure is an inevitable part of being human. We try hard at a job and get let go, we fall in love only to be left heartbroken, we try hard to live and sometimes life lets us down, or we say something hurtful that ends a friendship. These very understandable moments of failure are really what prove to us we are human. It doesn't mean that our failures will hurt any less. Let us be kind to ourselves and fail with grace.

> Close your eyes and bring to mind a moment you failed. As you breathe, invite in a sense of kindness to the moment.

285. OUR CALLING.

I never planned on being a meditation teacher. But it was my
calling, something that found me. My calling was undeniable.
When people ask how I found my career, I always say that it
found me. In college I always pursued journalism, which is what
I thought I wanted to do. I was driven by my mind. But medi-
tation called to my heart and soul, and I felt like I was coming
home. When I started teaching meditation, I knew my calling
had found me. It became so clear that every moment in my life
was leading me to that moment.

> Close your eyes and sense what your heart is called to do.
> What is something in your life that you are drawn to?
> Trust in this.

286. GET BACK UP.

Life defeats us and we lose hope, then we are rewarded and
shown moments of love. Let us no longer fear the defeat
and instead see it as an opportunity to get back up, stron-
ger and wiser. See, this is the unavoidable pain and beauty of
being human. We are constantly thrown challenges that bring
us to our knees. And in those moments, we are blessed with a
new beginning, and the chance to rise and begin again. Each
time the world knocks us down, let us see it as a moment of
awakening—a chance to get back up.

> Close your eyes and sense a challenge that you are
> currently struggling with. As you breathe, sense the
> strength in you to rise, heal, and learn.

287. HONESTY IN ANOTHER.

I'm lucky to have honest friendships where I can be fully myself without fear of being judged. My friends see me, hear me, and accept me as I am. As I grow spiritually, I realize the gift of truthfulness in others is better than friends who tell you what you want to hear. Friends who truly do have your best interest in mind will stick with you as you change, grow, and evolve, honoring you all the way through. These are friendships where your worth is never in question. Hold on to those friends closely, for they are one of life's beautiful gifts.

Close your eyes and bring to mind a friendship that is honest and true. As you breathe, send them love and appreciation. Rest in gratitude.

288. STAY.

We're so quick to rush to the next moment at times when our preferences aren't met in the present. It's hard to wait for love, for answers, or for another being to grow and change in the way you want them to. Our tendency is to jump ahead and seek answers in the future. But if we learn to stay in the moment and with what is, the answers will find us. We also must learn to stay with ourselves. When life gets hard and we feel sad, angry, or unworthy, we tend to self-abandon. But just as a parent would not leave a crying child, we should not leave ourselves. Let us stay.

Close your eyes and notice the mind's tendency to leave the present moment. Sense your body in the present. Let the mind stay present, too.

289. DO NOT FEAR CHANGE.

Sometimes change can be scary; it means being forced out of our comfort zones and leaving behind what we know. But change doesn't always have to be scary. Sometimes change is exactly what we need to learn and evolve into who we are meant to become. When my mother passed away, my life changed significantly. It weighed heavy on my heart, and I was scared to live life without a mother. But looking back, that change taught me about life and loss, giving me the courage to continue on. My fear then transformed into wisdom and allowed me to welcome in change.

Center yourself and bring to mind a change that is causing fear to rise in you. As you breathe, sense the wisdom growing inside of you.

290. BEING CLEAR.

Before we do something, let us investigate why we want to do it. Let us uncover the intention behind our actions. Seeking clarity in our intentions can help guide us to advocate for ourselves and act truthfully. Oftentimes we get distracted and consumed by fear-based opportunities or insecurities that deter us from what we truly want. Let our intentions clarify what we truly want. Let us give ourselves the gift of being clear about what we want so others can understand how to respond. By giving ourselves this gift, we show up in the world authentically.

Close your eyes and sense what you are about to do. As you breathe, ask yourself why you want to do it. Advocate for yourself today.

291. KNOW WHAT YOU DESERVE.

In knowing what we deserve, we can better voice our needs
and wants and be our own cheerleaders when reaching for our
goals. We should always remember that we deserve the world,
and are worthy of whatever it is that we desire. When we
know what we deserve, the journey becomes more enjoyable.
Rather than being caught up in what we don't yet have, we
can remember what we deserve and realize it's not a matter
of "if" but "when." Let us remember that we can do it and
we deserve it.

May I remember that I am worthy and deserving of it all.
May I remember that I can do anything I set my mind
and heart on.

292. LEADING WITH LOVE.

When we lead with love, we allow ourselves and others to be
courageous and honest and show up truthfully. We are free
from judgment and hate, and are filled with the understanding
and kindness that transforms any tough situation. When we
lead with love, we inspire others to lead with love as well. By
leading with love, we demonstrate its healing powers through
our actions and way of being. We reflect back the love inside
ourselves to remind others of their own love. Let us lead with
love and kindness and be love and kindness.

May I live life with love. May I live free of judgment and
hate. May I lead with love and hope that others will do
the same.

146

293. MOVING FORWARD.

We should all practice moving forward with grace and ease when life gets us down. In moving forward with a wise heart full of understanding—instead of a heavy heart full of resentment—we learn the beauty of resilience. We are able to stress less about the falling down and missteps on our journey, and can shed light on what we learned and how we got back up. Let us learn to move forward so that when life feels heavy, we know we have the power to transform. When we tap into the power and beauty of moving forward, we can conquer anything.

When life gets me down, may I move forward. May I move forward with grace and ease. May I know I am resilient.

294. RELEASING JUDGMENT.

When we release judgment, we feel lighter. Judgment feels heavy, whether we are being judged or are the ones judging others. Let us learn to transform judgment into understanding. Judgment often stems from a feeling of isolation and separation. But when we remember that we're all humans doing the best we can in the given moment, we can meet another with love and understanding. Let us release judgment so we can be free from the shackles of aloneness and come together in kindness and love. We must not let judgment deter us from our nature, which is loving and kind.

May I release the judgment I impose on others. May I release the heaviness when I feel judged. May I let go of judgment and be free.

295. UNLEARNING.

Life is not only about learning new things, but also unlearning old ways of being. So many of us inherit qualities and traits from the people who raised us, and the environments in which we grew up. While some of these qualities might be lovely, others may not be. It is never too late to unlearn. Let us learn to let go of who we think we're supposed to be, and how society has defined us to make space for the ever-changing nature of our existence. Let us peel away the layers, and shed what no longer serves us, to make space for who we want to be.

May I have the courage to unlearn parts of others I may have absorbed. May I make space to create the version of myself I wish to become.

296. DISAGREEMENTS.

Disagreements are a natural part of life. It is impossible to live a life free of disagreements. So, let us embrace that not everyone will have the same opinions as us. Oftentimes disagreement evokes a defensive response. But if we can meet others who don't share our beliefs with more compassion and understanding, we make space for a more loving environment. We can use disagreements to inspire compassion within ourselves and realize that disagreements do not mean that someone is against us. We can lean into our differences and accept them. Let us learn to meet disagreements as an opportunity to learn.

Close your eyes and bring to mind the last time you were in a disagreement with another. As you breathe, let go of your defenses.

297. THE WAY WE MAKE OTHERS FEEL.

The way we make others feel is often a reflection of how we feel about ourselves. Let us be the reason someone feels loved and worthy, rather than insecure or inferior. Let's build people up and remind them of their beauty and potential. But let us remember, too, that we can only remind others of what we know ourselves. So, let us remember that we are whole, loved, and worthy of it all. Let us show others how we feel and reflect it back to them. Let our happiness make others feel happy.

May I remember that I am loved and worthy. May I remind others that they are loved and worthy. May I make them feel whole.

298. BE JOYFUL ANYWAY.

When life gets tough, be joyful anyway. Sometimes when life is chaotic, it can almost feel wrong to crack a smile. But it is in those tough moments when joy is needed the most. Joy reminds us that even in the midst of suffering we can find reasons to smile. During times of crisis we can be thankful for the air in our lungs and the beating of our hearts. In the times when our health takes a turn for the worse, we can be grateful for the roof over our heads. Let life remind you to be joyful anyway. You have the power to define your state in the current moment.

Close your eyes and sense how you feel in the moment. As you breathe, choose joy anyway. See how your choice shifts how you feel.

299. OUR WORDS CAST A SPELL.

We must be mindful of the words we use in our thoughts and the words we speak aloud. Shaman Durek said, "Our words cast a spell." What we think and say manifests in our lives. So, if our struggle is anger, let us think of joy and speak joyfully. If our struggle is lack of abundance, let us think and speak abundantly. If we struggle with self-love, let our thoughts and words about ourselves be loving. Let us give our attention and energy to what it is that we want and cast that spell into the world.

May I understand that what I think and say is what manifests in my life. May I think kind and loving thoughts about myself and the world.

300. THINGS ARE AS THEY ARE.

We suffer when we wish things were different from the way things are. We suffer when our preferences aren't met. The secret to peace, then, is the acceptance of things as they are. We plan a beach day, and then it rains. We show up to the movie theater, and then the tickets are sold out. In both moments our immediate reaction may be anger, annoyance, and dissatisfaction. We may be unable to accept things as they are. But when we can begin to look at life and accept each moment as it is, our experience becomes easier and we suffer less.

Close your eyes and sense the moment as it is. As you breathe, allow yourself to accept the moment fully, letting go of preferences and judgment.

301. OUR CHANGING SELVES.

When I was a child, I remember hating classical music. As an adult I've grown to love it. When I was a child, I hated Brussels sprouts, and today it's one of my favorite vegetables. Just as our tastes in music and food shift, so do our minds, hearts, and souls. So much suffering arises when we try to label our evolving selves to fit into a tiny box, and seek confirmation and validation that we are a certain way. Let us embrace our changing selves; let us transcend our identity.

Close your eyes and sense the many selves you have been in the past. As you breathe, welcome in the many selves you will become.

302. DEEP LISTENING.

So often in my life I've turned to relationship books, podcasts, and advice from friends when I'm uncertain about what is happening in love, when all that is needed is to deeply listen to my heart. Or perhaps we've been the one quick to offer advice, rather than simply be present and listen with kindness. When we are unable to listen, we get caught up in projecting what it is we desire rather than seeing the moment or another as they actually are. Let us all learn to practice deep listening to others and ourselves. When we practice deep listening, we get closer to the truth.

Close your eyes and allow your awareness to land in the heart. As you breathe, practice deeply listening to the heart. What is it saying?

303. THE BUSYNESS OF LIFE.

How easy it is to get stuck on the hamster wheel of life, feeling like the days are endless and lead to nowhere. Sometimes when I think about life deeply, I feel overwhelmed, lost in a sea of 7 billion people, questioning whether or not my existence means anything. But then I think of a colony of ants, which looks to us like a bunch of little black dots on a pile of dirt. But each of these ants has an important role. It is the same with us; we humans are like the cells that make up the body, important pieces of the whole.

Center yourself and imagine you are a cell in a body, small but necessary for life to exist. With each breath, feel your connection to the whole.

304. DO NOT RUN FROM THE TRUTH.

The truth can hurt, and that is why so many of us run from it. Running from the truth might prolong feeling joy, peace, or love, but running will not lead to healing. Resist the urge to run from the truth; it is here to teach you. For so long I avoided the sadness that lived in my heart after my mother passed. I would lie to myself and others saying her passing made me stronger. I would drink, study, and constantly seek attention from others instead of facing the truth of sadness inside of me. The moment I stopped running, healing began.

Close your eyes and sense the truth that lives in your heart. Allow the heart to open fully, and meet whatever feelings arise. Do not run.

305. TRYING.

The famous saying "If at first you don't succeed, try, try again" is one of the most valuable lessons I have ever learned. Living by this lesson is easy as a kid, like when we fall off the bike and get back on and try again. But as we grow older, this advice becomes more difficult to follow. As adults we risk embarrassment, judgment, failure, and rejection, but that shouldn't stop us from trying. Let us embrace childlike fearlessness. Let us know that even in moments we're unsure of how things will begin, how they will go, or how they'll turn out, we should take the risk to try, try again.

If at first, I don't succeed, may I try again. May I see the beauty in trying, for if I don't try, I'll never know.

306. FACE WHAT SCARES YOU.

So many times I've lied through my teeth to avoid the difficult conversations or hurting someone's feelings. For many years I was a chronic people pleaser, thinking I was doing the right thing by trying to keep others happy. But as I've grown spiritually, I've learned the importance of facing the moments that scare me, speaking the truth even if it does hurt, and having the difficult conversations that need to be had for the greater good of humanity. We must face what scares us in order to live in our truth. We must face what scares us in order to make a difference.

Close your eyes and bring to mind a truth that you want to share but are afraid to. As you breathe, invite in the courage to speak up.

307. WOUNDS AND SCARS.

We must learn to wear our scars and not our wounds. So many of my students walk around, identifying with the difficulties and trauma that has happened to them. I am guilty of this, too. In college I assumed the identity of the sad and anxious girl who partied too much because she lost her mother. I wore my wounds. But as I healed, I learned to wear my scars instead. Then I walked with the wisdom and healing I learned from my wounds, and not the wounds themselves.

Breathe in, aware of your wounds. Breathe out the strength to heal. Realize you are so much more than what happened to you. Wear your scars.

308. LOVE IS A MOMENT AWAY.

When I was in Bali leading a retreat, we went to a school started by Westerners for children with learning disabilities. In Bali there is no care or schooling for these children due to a cultural belief that these children were born with disabilities because of their karma in a past life. When we arrived at the school, I broke down in tears. These children were full of joy and so tapped into love, even though they had been shunned by their families and communities. It reminded me that love is only a moment away. The love is always there. We just have to look.

May I know that when I can't find love outside myself, I can always find it inside. Love lives in my heart, waiting to be found.

309. GOING BACK ON OUR WORD.

My dad used to tell me to never go back on my word. He would say that if I've made a commitment, I should stick to it no matter what. I do see the truth in this. But as I've grown spiritually, I've realized that if sticking to my word puts my well-being at stake, it's okay to put my own happiness first. If it increases our happiness, going back on our word is an act of honoring ourselves. My teacher would say it's better to grace someone with your absence rather than your presence full of resentment.

Close your eyes and make a promise to yourself to honor your own happiness and well-being. Know that it's okay to cancel plans.

310. DANGER AND OPPORTUNITY.

As a child and teen, I was an avid horseback rider. I remember my parents would always hold their breath whenever I jumped because they had heard the horror stories of horseback riding injuries. I think the element of danger is what intrigued me about the sport. The adrenaline rush felt exciting, even though I knew I could break my neck or die in an instant. I thank horseback riding because it reminded me to not live in fear. There is always danger in life but also always opportunity. We just have to know what to look for.

Close your eyes and bring to mind something that excites you, but also scares you. As you breathe, allow both feelings to be there. Both are welcome.

311. TO HONOR ANOTHER.

How lucky we are to experience life alongside other beings, to hear of another experience here on earth that is not just your own. As I grew spiritually, I came to the realization that it is a gift to honor another's journey and experience, even if it is nothing like your own. However much we think we know about a person, we can never truly know what is going on in another's inner world. We must learn to honor other people's journeys, and bow to the uniqueness of who they are and what they are going through. Let us honor another so they can shine.

May I honor another and allow them to be who they are. I understand I will never fully understand, but still hold space.

312. PLANNING.

I've always been a chronic planner. In high school I remember being so worried on a Monday about what my weekend plans were that one of my friends told me to calm down, reminding me there was time. Of course we must make plans to show up to work, to go to bed, but oftentimes overplanning causes suffering. We become so attached to the outcomes that when our plans don't go as we expect, we suffer. We must learn to see the beauty and usefulness of planning, but perhaps let go of the expectation of things going exactly as we envision.

Close your eyes and bring to mind any plans you've made for the near future. As you breathe, soften and allow the plans to unfold as they may.

313. CONFUSION.

Confusion is dizzying. We get overwhelmed with too much information or not enough. We try to find clarity in the midst of not knowing the answers to our questions. I used to look at confusion as something bad, a state that I had to escape. But I'm learning now that there is beauty in not knowing answers yet; there is beauty in waiting for the answers to find you. Sometimes when I am confused, I prematurely jump to conclusions or make rash decisions to no longer feel the discomfort of confusion. But there is wisdom in the discomfort; sometimes waiting is necessary.

Close your eyes and bring to mind a situation that has you feeling confused. Allow yourself to rest there without trying to figure anything out.

314. CRYING.

I used to view crying as something only for the weak. But tears are a sign of strength. Tears are a sign of the heart breaking open to life. Recently I was out to dinner with one of my best girlfriends. She asked what some of my favorite memories of my mother were. I shared some favorite memories as well as some of the tougher ones. She gave me the space to share, cry, and release. Crying always reminds me of how important it is to feel my feelings. It reminds me of my strength.

Center yourself and bring to mind the last time you cried. As you breathe, allow yourself to sense the release and strength in that moment.

315. BEING STUBBORN.

In being stubborn, we put ourselves through unnecessary suffering to prove our rightness. We stand our ground, we try to prove our point, and we refuse to see something from another point of view. But as I grow spiritually, I'm realizing it's less important to be right than to be open-minded and flexible. Instead of being so rigid in our thoughts and set in our ways, let us be open to new ways. Let us be less stubborn, more open, and flexible. Because more often than I'd like to admit, I'm usually humbled and pleasantly surprised when I open up to what is new.

> Close your eyes and sense where you are being stubborn and close-minded. As you breathe, sense your tight grip on your view softening and becoming flexible.

316. OUR LIMITATIONS.

Far too often I used to let my limiting beliefs stop me from accomplishing my dreams. Even writing this book was something I thought would be impossible if you had asked me about it last year. I would have said, "I'm not a strong writer." Before I found boxing, I would have said, "I'm not athletic or strong." And now I'm in the best shape I've ever been. The point I'm trying to make is to let go of the mind's illusion of limitation. Our limiting beliefs hold us back from the magic that is possible. Let go of limitations and see what you can create.

> Close your eyes and notice what limiting beliefs you have. As you breathe, let go of these limiting beliefs and know that you can accomplish greatness.

317. SEEKING.

I found meditation after my mother passed when I was seeking answers about why her life had to be taken so young, to understand the way the universe worked. Before I found meditation, I was so sure of the way things worked and why things were the way they were (like many self-assured teenagers). But when my mother died, all that I thought was certain was proven not to be so. In discovering meditation, I became a seeker of truth, full of curiosity and wonder. As I grow in my spiritual journey, the one thing I know is that I know nothing at all.

May I remain curious and open. May I let go of what I think I know to be certain. May I be a seeker of truth.

318. WONDER.

Meditation and mindfulness reawakened my sense of wonder. As adults we seem to forget this, and we are less excited by life, as if we already know what it is all about. But mindfulness taught me to look at life in a whole new way. It taught me to meet each moment with curiosity, reminding me that each moment was one I had not yet experienced. Mindfulness reawakened my mind and heart. It was like life went from black and white to technicolor. All we have to do is meet each moment with a sense of wonder, and we will awaken to life.

Close your eyes and sense the air against the skin. Notice sounds as they appear and dissolve. Notice sensations in the body as they come and go.

319. SHEDDING OUR SKIN.

As we humans evolve and grow, a shedding of who we were is a necessary part of evolving into who we are becoming. I read a poem once called "Unbecoming" and used the word not in a negative way, but to describe the beauty of peeling the layers to reveal who we really are. Unbecoming who we were, and becoming who we are and will be, is like a snake shedding its skin. It is necessary to let go of who we were in order to fully be who we presently are.

> Close your eyes and allow yourself to unbecome. Allow yourself to peel away the layers of who you were, like a snake shedding its skin.

320. THE WHOLENESS OF YOU.

We are wondrous creatures. As Walt Whitman said, we contain multitudes. Let us learn to love all of ourselves. Let us love all the parts that make us whole. Let us love the creativity, the kindness, and the love. Let us love the anger, the boredom, and the sadness. Let us love every part of being human. Too often I've tried to amplify parts of myself that I thought were desirable, and silence qualities I thought others would find unattractive. But I've realized that what makes one most attractive is the ability to love oneself fully. To love every part of the whole.

> Center yourself and sense all the parts that make up the whole of your being. As you breathe, realize that every part is important and loveable.

321. THE RISK OF SEPARATION.

The feelings of isolation and being separate will weigh so heavy on the heart that it breaks. One of the most fundamentals needs of being human is a sense of belonging. Growing up I thought that being an independent individual who didn't need anybody was the sign of success. But now I know the true sign of success is to truly feel like I belong, and to feel safe, wanted, and loved by my friends, family, and community. Although there is nothing wrong with being alone or independent, tread lightly. The heart blossoms and thrives when it belongs.

Close your eyes as you sense where you feel separate. As you breathe, imagine the breath and sense that you belong, to yourself and to the world.

322. CLEANSE YOUR MIND.

Our minds love to overthink. It does us no good to ruminate or worry. Sometimes we need to cleanse our minds of thoughts that begin to consume us. I remember when my father had back surgery, I began to fear the idea of his death. My father was all I had, having already lost my mother and being an only child. I began to obsess over the idea of having to live life alone. For days after his surgery I lived in constant fear of his death, and my mind was consumed with worrisome thoughts. But this worrying did me no good; it only caused me suffering.

Close your eyes and as you breathe, notice the worrisome thoughts that consume your mind. Let them all go. Cleanse your mind.

323. ALONE TOGETHER.

So often in experiencing difficulties we feel alone. I remember having crippling anxiety attacks and thinking that no one understood. I remember falling so deeply into grief after my mom passed that it left me feeling isolated and misunderstood. But the thing to remember is that we are never alone. Yes, the causes and conditions for our suffering may be very different, but when it comes down to it, every human has experienced a similar suffering. This notion that we're not alone in our suffering brings me peace. Let us remember that when we feel alone, we are alone together.

> Center yourself and sense any difficulties weighing on the heart. As you breathe, know that you are not alone. You are alone, together, with all beings.

324. HONEST EXPRESSION.

Being honest, not only with others but also with ourselves, is valuable and necessary. We must be honest with ourselves about how we feel. I used to think setting boundaries was difficult, but now I clearly see boundaries are just an expression of the love we have for ourselves. Honesty in another is a gift, too. I respect my friends who tell me how they feel and express their needs and desires, because I view it as their own expression of the love they have for themselves.

> Close your eyes and recall a time you did not express your true desires. Remember how that felt. As you breathe, make a promise to be honest.

325. THE NEED TO BE ACCEPTED.

All humans have the desire to be accepted. A sense of belonging is necessary for our well-being. As a kid in elementary school, I remember wanting to be accepted by the "cool" kids. My parents would tell me that this feeling goes away when you become an adult. But this need still exists in me today. From high school to college, then to work, this need to belong is something that will be with us forever. It's not something to be ashamed of, but rather a quality to be nurtured. Let us all find people and communities that make us feel like we belong.

> Close your eyes and bring to mind a time when you felt like you truly belonged. As you breathe, remember you deserve to feel like you belong.

326. THE ONLY WAY OUT IS IN.

I remember struggling as a child and teen to fit in, to be some imagined perfect image of "popular" or "cool." But the moment I fully embraced who I was instead of what I thought people wanted me to be, I found peace. I wanted out of my "uncool" and "nerdy" ways, but the only way out was to fully embrace all of who I was. The only way out is in. The only way to get to where you want to go is to be who you really are. I turned inward, and learned to love every part of myself.

> Close your eyes and sense the part of yourself you are trying to escape. As you breathe, reach in and love that part of yourself.

327. DEDICATION AND POSSIBILITY.

When we are dedicated to our heart's full opening, all is possible. For so many years I didn't allow my heart to fully open. I would only show parts of myself, in hopes that another being would find me likeable, afraid that if I fully opened my heart I would be rejected. But I'm learning that by fully opening our hearts, we discover who and what is really worth our time and affection. Let our existence be dedicated to the full blossoming of the heart. Let our heart show us what is truly possible.

> May my existence be a dedication to my heart's full opening. May those I surround myself with fully embrace me and what I have to offer.

328. THE SURPRISES AND GIFTS OF BEING HUMAN.

Life is so fragile yet so magical. When I think of my mom's life and death, both the fragility of life and the gift of life become so clear. Her death showed me that life is short and tomorrow isn't promised. But the way she lived, showed me life's magic. From the way she met my dad to how they spent their retirement and traveled the world, to my adoption and the way she raised me—everything showed me the universe had a plan. We are shown that life is fragile, death is imminent, and magic is possible.

> Close your eyes and sense the fragility of life. As you breathe, sense the magic and divinity within you. Embrace the surprises and gifts of being human.

329. TAKE A CHANCE.

After my mom passed, I traveled alone to Peru. I had initially planned the trip with my boyfriend at the time, but right before the trip he broke up with me. I knew it was a sign from the universe that I had to take a chance. It's the best chance I ever took. I was scared beyond belief but had a deep inner-knowing that it was needed. I trusted that I would be safe. I trusted that I would find my way, see what I needed to see, and learn what I needed to learn. I took a chance, trusted, and am so glad I did.

Center yourself and sense a chance you are afraid to take. As you breathe, trust that you are guided and that everything will happen as it should.

330. AWAKEN AWE.

Before I found meditation and spirituality, I used to complain so much. I'd complain about the weather, complain about other people's actions or words, complain about work, complain about material possessions, and so much more. When my mother passed, all of that changed. I realized what a gift being alive is. Meditation taught me the magic of the present moment. Spirituality taught me to trust in the magic of the universe. I awakened to life and began to truly live in each moment. Life teaches us to awaken to the beauty in every moment, the beauty inside of us, and in the world.

May I awaken to life's beauty. May I awaken to the beauty inside myself. May I awaken to the magic of each and every moment.

331. UNDERSTANDING.

When we care for ourselves, we care for the world, and when we care for the world, we care for ourselves. Compassion and understanding are qualities that meditation helped me cultivate. I learned that by caring for my own wounds, I help myself heal and transform. When meditation helped me meet the grief from the loss of my mother with kindness, I began to heal. Now when I meet others who have experienced the loss of another, there is a part of my heart that is similar to the heart of that other person. Compassion and understanding connects us to others, and to the world.

> Close your eyes and recall a time you met a friend with a kind and understanding heart. Sense the similarities in both your hearts.

332. GRATITUDE.

It's very easy to become aware of our wants, needs, and desires. We become so fixated on a goal that we miss the beauty around us in the here and now. One of my teachers once described gratitude as a "having in the midst of not having." We recognize what's already beautiful in our lives. Often when we rest in gratitude long enough, we begin to appreciate not only the joyful moments, but also the tough moments. The moments that broke us down, after which we got back up—the moments we were reminded of our courage and resilience.

> Today, may I recognize what is already beautiful in my life. May I savor what makes me smile, and what makes my heart feel full.

333. A NEW DAY.

Every day we are given the gift of 24 brand-new hours to live, breathe, be, and exist. We are starting the day with a refreshed mind, heart, and pair of eyes through which we see the world. Sometimes we get bogged down by our own suffering as well as the world's. We go to sleep worrying and wake up worrying. But this worrying diminishes our chances for joy. An energy healer once told me to allow the night and my slumber to clear my energetic state, and to start the next day anew. Let the new day refresh you.

> As you go to sleep, put your worries to rest. When you wake up, take in the gift of a brand-new day and of being alive.

334. SINCERITY.

Let us be sincere in our living, being, and doing. Let us live in our truth and see the truth in others. As I grow spiritually, I can always sense when I am being insincere. I sense my body tense up when I say "yes," but I really want to say "no." I sense the emptiness in doing tasks that do not fill my heart with love and joy. Our hearts are always guiding us on a journey of truth, and when we are insincere, our bodies will tell us. Let us live a sincere life, and let it be magic.

> Close your eyes and sense what the heart wants. Sense the truth in this message. Let your day be filled with following your heart.

335. THE GIFT OF RELATIONSHIP.

To be in relationship with another, romantically or not, is one of the magical gifts of our human experience. To be able to be fully seen and heard without judgment by another is freeing. Every day we put on a façade. We do what we think others want or need, we strive to be likeable and accepted, we act in ways that we believe will be rewarded. Not that any of this is bad, but there is a sense of freedom when you can take off your façade and be your true, authentic self and are celebrated for it.

Center yourself and take off whatever façade you have on. Recall and send love to anyone in your life who loves you without your façade.

336. WHAT WE CHERISH.

To know what you love and cherish is a wonderful, priceless skill. You are given the secret toolbox to your own happiness. When I feel sad, unworthy, angry, or uncomfortable, I know I can turn to my favorite people, activities, or wisdom to fill my heart. Find what you love and do it often. Surround yourself with the people you love, those who reflect back to your own greatness. Read the books, buy the crystals, and take the classes that light you up. For what you cherish will remind you that you are worthy of being cherished.

Close your eyes and bring to mind the activities or people you cherish. Sense how this cherishing makes you feel. You, too, are worthy of being cherished.

337. THE GIFT OF DREAMS.

Dreams are the gateway to what is possible. My mom passed almost 10 years ago, and I still dream of her. In my dreams she is so alive, just like I remember her. Her smile, her laugh, and her eyes are all very much alive. I'm grateful for these dreams because they remind me that even though my mom isn't phys- ically alive, she is still very much alive in my mind and heart. Dreams have this magical power to awaken the essence of what you desire. Dreams don't always reflect reality, but they teach us and show us what our soul needs to see.

Close your eyes and bring to mind a dream that really stuck with you. What did it teach you? What did your soul need to learn?

338. YOU ARE THE AUTHOR OF YOUR STORY.

We are the creators of our own lives. I could have so easily fallen victim to the story of a sad girl who had no mother, who would get married without a mom to see it, and have kids with no grandmother. After my mom passed, I saw that the choice was up to me. Today, I live the story I created. A woman who loves her mom physically but is divinely guided by her spirit. A woman who uses the loss of her mother to teach others the gifts of meditation. A woman who will get married and have kids with her mom watching over her.

Center yourself and bring to mind the story of your life. What story are you writing? As you breathe, feel your power to create.

339. WELCOMING WITHOUT JUDGMENT.

Let us learn to welcome emotions without judgment. Humans are judgmental, so it does take a little effort to let go of our tendency to name feelings, people, places, and situations as "good" or "bad." It's the added layer of judgment that tends to affect our experience. I used to view the anxiety that arose in me as "bad," and it made my experience quite unpleasant. I would push it away, try to numb it, or run from it. Mindfulness taught me to meet emotions with curiosity and kindness, so when anxiety arises, I now become curious and my experience is fluid and manageable.

> Close your eyes and sense all the emotions arising within you. Meet them without judging them as good or bad. Invite them in with kindness and curiosity.

340. PASSION AND PURPOSE.

There is a word in Japanese called *ikigai* that means "reason for being." I remember learning about ikigai in a TED talk about the Blue Zones, the areas of the world where people live the longest. One thing they all had in common was a reason for being. If we love what we do, work will never feel like work; it will just feel like life. My career fulfills both my needs of awakening passion inside of me and serving a purpose, and increasing peace and well-being in myself and all beings I teach. Let us find our passion and purpose.

> Close your eyes and ask the heart, "What fills you with passion?" Ask yourself, "What passion of mine will serve the greater good of all beings?"

341. THE PURSUIT.

Let us learn to look at facing obstacles as the pursuit of greatness. I used to think obstacles were a blockage to my happiness. When I changed my perspective to viewing obstacles as a stepping-stone to magic, my life began to change. The toughest moments in my life have built me into the woman I am today. If life were only easy, I wouldn't be as strong, courageous, or compassionate as I am today. I thank the obstacles for teaching me to step into my power and own who I am. Let our obstacles inspire us to pursue greatness.

Close your eyes and bring to mind any obstacles you are currently facing. As you breathe, begin to see them as stepping-stones to you pursuing greatness.

342. THE UNSEEN.

Some of the best things in life are unseen. Love and truth are described in poems, plays, movies, art, and books, but even those works of art cannot compare to the feelings in the heart. Both love and truth, when felt in the heart, awaken us to life. It's those moments we feel love in our hearts and the truth in our souls when we truly know what it's like to be alive. So let the unseen parts of life excite you, let them break you, let them build you back up. There is so much more to life than what meets the eye.

Close your eyes and sense the love in your heart. As you breathe, feel the truth in your soul. Trust that what you cannot see is magic.

343. BREAKING THROUGH.

I come so much closer to the full experience of life when I break through the image of what I think society wants me to be. I break through my ideas of who I think I need to be in order to be lovable. I break through the façade I put up of what I think is needed to be likeable and accepted. I break through to my true self, into who I really am, and into who I am becoming. Let us break through our ideas of who we think we should be, and allow our authentic selves to emerge into life.

Close your eyes and sense the ways that your true and authentic self feels trapped. As you breathe, break through into who you really are.

344. IDENTITY.

Who we are is fluid and changing. I've evolved from child to teen to adult. I've transformed from doing ballet and playing violin to horseback riding to boxing. I have witnessed my journey from innocent child, to angsty teen, to responsible adult. Our identity is a bunch of moving parts that in one particular moment is how we see ourselves and how we present ourselves to the world. Let us not confine who we are to one word or label or try and fit it inside a box. Let us invite in all of who we are, knowing that our identity is always changing.

Center yourself and sense who you are in this moment. Know that who you were yesterday is different from who you will be tomorrow.

345. BE RECEPTIVE TO OTHERS.

Let others in your life show up exactly as they are. I've found that I create so much of my own suffering when I expect a friend or lover or anyone in my life to show up in a certain way or I expect them to be something that they are not. I'm learning that when we allow people to show up as best they can in the moment, we create a space for authentic connections to grow and evolve. Let us be receptive to others and honor their journey and growth so that we can all awaken together.

Bring to mind a relationship that is upsetting you. Let go of how you want them to show up. Let them be as they are.

346. WHERE YOU CAN BE HARSH, BE SOFT.

We are so hard on ourselves. We tend to be our own worst enemies, rather than our own best friends. Let us learn to be kinder to ourselves. The voice inside our heads is always judging, telling us we could be doing more, working harder, being more active, etc. Our inner critic is constantly active. When we notice our inner critic chiming in, let us invite in our inner soother. When we could be hard, let us be soft. When we could be mean, let us be kind. At the end of the day all we have is ourselves, so let us be our own best friend.

Close your eyes and notice what the inner critic is saying. As you breathe, invite in your inner soother. Be soft, kind, and gentle with yourself.

347. WHAT WE RUN FROM.

We tend to run from what scares us. But what we run from is often our greatest teacher. Meditation taught me to stop running. It taught me that what I tend to run from is exactly the thing I need to face. I spent years running from sadness, afraid to feel what was building up after the loss of my mother. The moment I stopped running, I began to learn. Sadness was my greatest teacher and continues to teach me to this day. When I notice myself starting to think about running, I take it as a sign it's something I must face in order to grow.

> Center yourself and notice what feelings you're running from. As you breathe, stop running, and turn toward the feelings. See what they have to teach you.

348. HUMILITY.

The moments that bring us to the point of breakdown, tears, and feeling like we cannot continue on will often fuel the change we're looking for. Life humbles us in unexpected ways. My moments of heartbreak, embarrassment, and failure have truly been the moments that inspired me to get back up. The struggles really do make us stronger. We may not see the beauty in the breakdown in the moment, but when looking back on our journeys, those moments were necessary. They taught us what we needed to learn to continue on. Let life humble you. Let us walk on our path with humility.

> May I understand that life's toughest moments are humbling, teaching me to walk with wisdom and understand what being human is all about.

349. FREEDOM IN TRUTH.

There is so much freedom in the truth. When I was younger, I remember keeping secrets for my friends and from my friends and how it felt like those secrets would eat away at my soul. As I grow spiritually, I've learned that ultimate freedom rests in truth. Not only in telling the truth rather than a lie are we no longer withholding information, but we're also being truthful with ourselves. Too often I've found myself in relationships far beyond their deadline, lying to myself that maybe it will work out or the dynamic would change, when all that was needed was the freeing truth that this wasn't the right person.

Close your eyes and sense any truth you are withholding from yourself. As you breathe, see the full truth and let it in. Be free.

350. YOUR ESSENCE IS RARE.

Your essence is rare, and anytime someone wants you to change, don't. Anytime I begin to sense that someone or some situation is asking me to change and not be who I really am, I see it as a red flag. Our unique essence is our gift to this world. It's what sets you apart from the 7.8 billion people here on this earth. We should be honored and celebrated for that, not ashamed. Not only in your career, but also in love and life. Be who you are and hold nothing back. You are you, and that is your superpower.

Close your eyes and sense the essence of you. Sense its rarity, its uniqueness. As you breathe, celebrate your individuality. Let it shine bright.

351. HEALING OURSELVES.

We all carry wounds that sometimes heal quickly, and others that don't. This is all okay, because each of us has the ability to heal ourselves. The beautiful thing about meditation is that there's nothing we need to do except offer our presence to whatever pains we experience. Just as a wound needs air to heal, all we need is kindness, patience, and time. We simply sit with and be with our wounds, meet them with kindness, and then they'll begin to heal. We must honor what we encounter in life, and trust that we have the healing power within us.

Close your eyes, and sense whatever pains you carry in your heart. As you breathe, trust your ability to heal yourself. Your presence is medicine.

352. ENLIGHTENED MOMENTS.

One of my favorite teachings is that there are not enlightened beings, only enlightened moments. I love this so much because it takes the pressure off of me and fully acknowledges being human. Even after years of spiritual practice, I still experience my off days where I feel lots of anxiety and frustration. But then there are other days when I'm very equanimous and filled with ease, no matter what life brings. Let us wake up to the enlightened moments. Let us savor them. And on days we feel far from spiritual, let us love ourselves then, too, for an enlightened moment is another breath away.

Close your eyes and take in the magic of the moment. Feel the magic of life that surrounds you. Sense the peace and ease inside of you.

353. THE OBSERVER.

The beauty of meditation is that it shows us that we are the observers of our present moment experience. Before I found meditation, I used to become so enmeshed in my thoughts. Awareness gives us the space to take a step back and see thoughts, feelings, and sensations as they rise and fall. Awareness reminds us that we are the observers of our lives. Let us utilize this gift of observations so that we learn to respond instead of reacting, and learn the nature of our minds and hearts.

> Close your eyes and imagine yourself sitting on a riverbank, watching leaves float by gently on the water. This is you observing your life.

354. THE EYES OF A CHILD.

Let us learn to look at the world through the eyes of a child—unconditioned by society, unconcerned with the troubles of tomorrow, life, love, and jobs. Children have an innocence about them. They can go from crying to laughter in a moment's time. Children are our greatest teachers in remaining present in the moment. When we learn to look at the world as if looking through the eyes of a child, we see the newness of each moment. We let go of our worries of the day and see the magic in the little things. When we look at life in this way, it's a remembering of our joyful nature.

> Center yourself and rest in an open awareness, taking in the image of whatever is in front of you. Imagine yourself looking through the eyes of a child.

355. THINKING LESS.

The secret to peace is not thinking more, but rather thinking less. Just as life is to be lived and not understood, thinking less truly is the gateway to freedom. Let us unhook from our thinking minds and drop down into our hearts and bodies so we can live life. Experience is not something we think about, but rather something that is felt in the body and soul. Reading a book about traveling or thinking about traveling is not the same thing as getting on a plane and actually traveling. Let us think less and live more fully.

Close your eyes and notice the thoughts rising and falling. Drop out of the mind and into the body and feel life as it moves through you.

356. LET THE HEART BREAK.

Every human has experienced heartbreak, and for most of us it's extremely tough. When I experience heartbreak, in the moment I don't see the beauty it's preparing me for. But when I look back on heartbreak, I see that it was truly the medicine I needed. The heart will continue to break, even after we find our love or our person. Our hearts will break when a loved one dies, when we lose a job, or when a friendship ends. The heart breaks and breaks, breaking open into the fullness of life. So, let the heart break and know that it is preparing you for magic.

Recall the last time your heart broke. As you breathe, take in all the lessons that heartbreak has taught you. When the heart breaks, get ready for magic.

357. GIVING AND RECEIVING.

Our interaction with all things is a relationship of giving and receiving. We form symbiotic relationships with people, nature, work, and so much more. In our Western society we are so obsessed with consumption. Consumption of information, money, material items. We are so obsessed with consumption that we forget that life is about giving, too. I think that's why community has such a profound effect on the heart. When we give back to others, our own problems seem to leave us, and our heart is filled with kindness and generosity. Let us also be open to receiving from others. Let us learn to give and receive consciously.

Sense that as you breathe, the earth is giving you air and life. As you breathe, sense that you are giving the earth the gift of you.

358. APPRECIATIVE JOY.

I have a tattoo on my arm that represents this quality of appreciative joy, known as *Muditā*. It is a quality of rejoicing in the good fortune of another. One of my teachers at UCLA's Mindful Awareness Research Center once said something that stuck with me forever. She said that we think our true friends are the ones who stick with us through the tough times, but that really our true friends are the ones who can be happy for us when we succeed. So let us notice when others are happy for us, and let us celebrate our friends when they do well.

Take a moment to celebrate your own good fortune. The next time a friend tells you something exciting, celebrate them and their good fortune.

359. BEGINNING AGAIN.

Life is a constant beginning again. We begin again at a micro level, with each moment and breath, and we begin again in a macro level in life events. This may seem disheartening. Who wants to begin again when they've come so far? But this idea of beginning again is exciting to me. It's freeing because we are no longer defined by our past; we are given the chance to start again as a new version of us in a new moment. Even in meditation, when a thought arises, we are able to begin again with each new breath. Meditation is resilience training in the mind and in life.

With each breath, sense that you are beginning again, beginning anew. Our lives are like this new breath. Each moment we begin again.

360. LIFE HAS A WAY.

Life has a way of bringing exactly what we need to learn in perfect time. I remember the week before I decided to be sober. It was the eve of my 28th birthday, and I was drinking and getting into tiffs with my best girlfriends. One of my best friends told me I get mean when I drink. The next week I went on a silent retreat, did a cleanse, and realized I didn't ever want to drink again. That birthday, the silent retreat, and the cleanse all came in perfect time. My soul was ready to be sober, and life showed me the way.

Close your eyes and sense what life is trying to teach you. Notice what people are saying to you and how life is unfolding. Sense the synchronicity.

361. WANTING AND HAVING.

I find myself getting so distracted by what I want that I seem to forget what I have. I want more money, I want more love, I want more adventure. In this wanting, there is a clinging to something outside of ourselves and the present moment. In the midst of this wanting we should learn to remember what we already have. In the midst of wanting to meet my person and find true love, I must remember the love I have inside myself, and the love I have from my friends and family. Let us remember the beauty of what we have in the here and now.

> Close your eyes and sense your desires. As you breathe, remember what you already have—the air in your lungs and the love in your heart.

362. INTEGRITY.

In this spiritual journey, we learn to be honest with ourselves and to love ourselves unconditionally. We learn about and find clarity in our own morals, and understand the ethics of life. When we fuse spiritual teachings with the truthfulness of our lives, we live with integrity. Let us not only learn and do but also let us be. Let our expression of life be the greatest teacher to others. I remember that when I first learned about meditation, all I wanted to do was tell everyone to do it. I realized the best way to teach others was by living the life I was teaching about.

> Center yourself and sense the message that you want to share with the world. Rather than explain it, be it. Show it in the way that you are and the way that you live.

363. SPEAK YOUR TRUTH.

For so long I was afraid to share my story. I was afraid that telling people I was adopted, or that my mother had died, would deem me unlovable. But I've learned the power in speaking my truth and sharing my story. My story and what I've learned along the way is now my career. I've also learned the necessity of speaking truth in the moment. When we hold anything back, we help no one; we only harm ourselves. So, speak your truth. Share your story. Be fully you and hold nothing back.

Close your eyes and sense the truth in your heart of what you wish to express. Give yourself the gift of truth today.

364. IMPERMANENCE.

Everything changes, and nothing stays the same. This is true with the earth and with who we are. This is one of the most fundamental teachings in meditation, and it changed my life. My mother's death taught me that life is impermanent. My changing and aging body, changing feelings, and changing interests show me that I myself am impermanent. When relationships begin and end, it shows that other people are impermanent. The earth spins, and seasons change. When we can accept life's impermanent nature, we begin to experience freedom. Let us embrace life's changing and impermanent nature, and let it teach us to appreciate each moment.

Close your eyes and sense the life changing around us. Sense yourself changing. Contemplate life and death. Realize all is impermanent and you will be free.

365. PRESENCE.

To be fully present is to be fully you. Presence is a quality that will change your life. In fact, I determine the quality of my day not by how much I accomplish, but rather by how fully present I was. Let us learn to be more present. Let us learn to be with each breath as it rises and falls, with each sound as it comes and goes, with each sensation in the body reminding us we are alive. Let us be more present when we speak and listen to others. Let us live in the present moment; it's all we have.

Close your eyes and sense your body in the here and now. Become the observer of your present moment experience. You are in the here and now.

RECOMMENDED
READING

Radical Acceptance by Tara Brach

No Mud, No Lotus: The Art of Transforming Suffering by Thich Nhat Hanh

Peace Is Every Step by Thich Nhat Hanh

Real Love: The Art of Mindful Connection by Sharon Salzberg

Vibrate Higher Daily: Live Your Power by Lalah Delia

INDEX

ACKNOWLEDGMENTS

To my mother, Lourdes, who taught me all of life's lessons on strength and self-love in her years here on this planet, and who continues to teach me to believe and trust in something bigger in her years as my angel.

To my father, Jack, who continues to teach me gratitude and unconditional love every single day.

To my teacher and mentor of many years, Heather Prete. Thank you for teaching me to love my humanness and leading me down the path of mindfulness and Buddhism. Thank you for reflecting back to me my own inner goodness.

To my best friends, you know who you are. Thank you for witnessing me on my journey, for supporting me, and believing in me. It means the world.

ABOUT THE AUTHOR

 **Laurasia Mattingly** is a meditation and mindfulness instructor and Reiki master based in Los Angeles. After the loss of her mother, Laurasia experienced debilitating anxiety and spent years exploring her own spirituality. She discovered that her passion lies in teaching people to live by the way of the heart. Laurasia guides her students by sharing the tools to finding peace, joy, and ultimately happiness in the present moment. She is the founder of her own virtual meditation platform, The Sit Society, and leads retreats around the world.

CPSIA information can be obtained
at www.ICGtesting.com
Printed in the USA
JSHW041912050222
22584JS00002B/2

9 781647 399498